A Century of Paglesham Life

Zachary Pettitt
1838 - 1916

©
Angela Puzey
Rosemary Roberts

To our grandchildren,
David, Katie, Sally,
Rebecca, Matthew, and Jamie

ACKNOWLEDGEMENTS

We would like to thank very many people in Paglesham, and relatives of old Paglesham families, for their assistance with facts, figures and photographs. We are sorry it has not been possible to mention everyone or to be able to use all the material available. We must apologise to all those people who have played their vital parts in the life of the village over the past years, but to whom we have been unable to refer, due to lack of space. We are most grateful for all their help, without which the story of the last hundred years would be much less interesting.

We must, however, say thank you specifically to: the Evening Echo for allowing us to publish photos taken from the Southend Standard and for access to their early back numbers; the Essex Record Office for continuing assistance; Peter Thorogood for copying old photos; Ann Brown and Nicola Robinson for the typing; Allison Bond (nee Roberts) and Rodney Choppin for illustrations; Margaret Pinkerton, who has, once again, allowed us to use the Wiseman family diaries, etc, from which we have taken much information; Ian Puzey for proof reading; and last but by no means least, Mark Roberts, our kind and diligent editor for his guiding hand and assistance throughout the writing and preparation of this book.

Printed by Cambridge Press, Shoeburyness

Published by M A & R Roberts
Paglesham 1993

ISBN 0 9516370 1 0

CONTENTS	Page
The Centenary of 1893	1
PART 1	
Mission Room Opening	2
Zachary Pettitt	3
Paglesham in the 1890s	5
The Oyster Merchants	6
The Village	10
Victorian Life	25
The New Century	30
The Great War	35
Between the Wars	37
PART 2	
The War Years	46
Post-War Changes	51
The Fifties	55
The Sixties	64
The Seventies	67
The Eighties	71
Recent Years	78
Postscript	81
Sources	81
Index of Names	82
General Index	83

ILLUSTRATIONS

The Mission Room, by Allison Bond	Cover
Location plan of Paglesham	Inside
Zachary Pettitt, 1838 - 1916	i
The Mission Room and Buckland Cottages - c1910	1
Loftmans, Canewdon - c1929	4
The Chase, sale catalogue - 1903	7
James Foster Turner Wiseman, 1835-1903	8
Frederick John Wiseman, 1829-1897	8
Athelstan and Zillah Harris - c1903	9
Finches and Maules - c1910	11
Horse-drawn brakes outside the Punch Bowl - 1900s	11
Church Hall pond and the church - c1910	12
Paglesham School - c1895, (by Allison Bond, 1990)	14
Barges on the River Roach - c1910	16
The timberyard and thatched barn at boatyard - c1910	16
Hallowe'en in the boat shed - 1950, (R S Choppin 1987)	17
Oyster dredgermen, outside Plough & Sail - early 1900s	18
Milton Villa, New and Shop Row, Waterside Lane - c1910	18
Plough and Sail, sale catalogue - 1903	20
A charabanc and party outside Plough & Sail - c1919	21
The Chase, from the sale catalogue - 1903	21
The Hutley family, outside Cupola House - 1912	23
Rose Cottage, predecessor to 'Hove To' - c1910	23
Stannetts, (by R S Choppin, 1987)	24
Victorian costume, from a Wiseman scrapbook	25
Confirmation Card for Ella Mary Woolf - 1897	29
Paglesham Church, (by Allison Bond, 1980)	30
'The Trading Post', and Barn Row, East End - 1970s	32
Atkinsons shop, Church End, 1920	34
The Great War - Territorials - c1915	34
The No 10 bus - 1920s, (by Allison Bond, 1993)	38
WI Fete at Redcroft - 1933	39
Poster for WI Fete at Redcroft - 1933	40
Alan Boardman on Fordson, Mission Room behind - c1938	42
Fred Kemp and Ted May, near New Cottages - 1930s	42
Milk deliveries by Tom Wood - 1930s	42
Lol Bradley and Gwen Wood	47
2nd World War - Home Guard	47
Cover of VPA Schedule - 1947	52
WI Ration Book - 1940/1942	52
Harvesting at Church End - early 1950s	58
Early VPA Show - c1950	58
Pumping out floodwater, Vic Cardy and son - 1953	60
VPA Prizewinners - 1957	60
A snowy scene - the road past the Mission Room - 1958	63
WI Harvest Supper in the Mission Room - 1959	63
VPA Supper at the Plough and Sail - 1960	65
Regulars in the Plough & Sail - late 1960s	65
Miss Winnie Keeble's 80th Birthday - 1975	70
VPA Childrens party - 1983	72
VPA 40th Anniversary photo - 1986	73
WI meeting - 1986	73
Bazaar in aid of Mission Room Funds - 1990	77
Art Exhibition, Mission Room - 1992	77
WI 60th Celebration - 1993	80
Ian Puzey and Mark Roberts, Music Hall Evening - 1990	80
Map by J F T Wiseman, changes at East End - 1873	84
Harvesting, old and new, (Modern combine by Allison Bond, 1993)	Back cover

THE CENTENARY OF 1893

The corrugated iron hall at East End, Paglesham, has played an important part in village life for a hundred years.

We have written this book to celebrate the Centenary of the 'Mission Room', as it has always been called, and as a 'Thank You' to Zachary Pettitt, who gave it to the village in 1893. He was a great benefactor in many ways both to Paglesham and to Canewdon, where he lived from 1878, but Paglesham seems to have been his first love. For example, he and James F T Wiseman - the two churchwardens - were the moving forces in the restoring our church in 1883.

Zachary Pettitt died in 1916, but he would have seen, by then, how much the Mission Room was used; for services, entertainments and as a Reading Room. We are sure he would be pleased at its continued use for a variety of activities, many unknown to him, over the years - for Men's, and Boys' Clubs, the Women's Institute, the Village Produce Association, Whist Drives, Harvest Suppers, parties, keep fit, and in recent years a flourishing art class.

The Mission Room and Buckland Cottages - c1910

In Part 1 of this book we have tried to show what the village was like a hundred years ago, and some of the changes and events up to the Second World War. Part 2 chronicles the life of the village since then, through the activities held in the Mission Room, with other aspects of the village as background.

PART 1

MISSION ROOM OPENING

"Saturday, 15th July 1893 saw a great celebration in the small village of Paglesham at the opening of the Parish Room", as the event was described at the time in one of the local papers.

"The 'East End' of Paglesham presented a scene of much animation on Saturday evening upon the occasion of the formal opening of the Mission-room, which has been presented to the parish by Mr Zachary Pettitt. The building abuts on the highway, and, in addition to defraying the entire cost of its erection, Mr Pettitt also provided the site upon which it stands. It is capable of seating 150 persons; and it is constructed of corrugated iron (externally) and match-boarding (internally). The contract was given to Mr N Kemp, of Rochford, who carried out the work in a manner which has given every satisfaction. The room will be used for Church services, entertainment, and meetings; and it is also proposed to establish in connection with it a parochial library. A Communion table has been placed at one end of the room for use at religous services; but, by a somewhat novel arrangement, it can easily be shut up and obscured from view when not required. For many years past the want of such a building has been greatly felt in the parish, and, it need scarcely be said, the inhabitants deeply appreciate the generosity of Mr Pettitt. In celebration of the event, a public tea was held; and it was very largely attended by parishioners and others. Flags were flying at several of the houses, and over the door of the mission-room was the motto, "All health and happiness to Mr and Mrs Pettitt and family." The tea was of a most substantial character, and it was served in a tent and in the Mission-room, both of which were crowded. Amongst those who acted as carvers and waiters, or rendered assistance in other ways, were Mrs Pettitt, Miss Mortier, Mrs Lea, the Misses Wiseman, Mrs Quy, Miss Quy and several gentlemen. A small charge was made for the tea, towards which some joints and other eatables were sent by Mr & Mrs Pettitt, Mrs Winterbon of Rochford also kindly contributed to the visitors' table."

At a combined meeting and concert that was held in the tent afterwards, the Rector (Rev Thomas Lea) made a "*genial chairman*" and after his speech of thanks to Mr Pettitt, "*an interesting presentation was next made to Mr Pettitt, in recognition of his kindness, and to mark the esteem that is entertained for him. The idea of the presentation originated quite spontaneously with the parishioners, and the necessary funds were soon forthcoming. The money was devoted to purchasing a massive tray of the best silver-plate, and also a handsome cake basket. These were accompanied by a suitable address, bearing the names of the subscribers, who numbered about 150. The prime movers in connection with the matter Messrs Harry Kemp, Alfred Kemp and William Woolf.*"

After thanks from Mr Pettitt and more speeches, the Rural Dean, the Rev T O Reay said "*he was convinced that the Mission-room would be a great boon, more especially during the winter evenings, which seemed so long...*"

"*The musical programme was then proceeded with. A pleasing variety of songs were sung by Miss Gertrude James, the Misses Quy, Mr Arthur Wiseman, Mr Hector Pettitt, Mr W Hill and Mr Sidney Baldwin (of Southend). The latter gentleman was encored for one of Chevalier's coster songs. A pianoforte duet was played by Mr L Quy and Miss P Wiseman; and a pathetic recitation was given by Mr Wilfred Beckwith.*"

After more thanks, "*the National Anthem was sung; and Mr Pettitt and Mrs Pettitt and their friends drove away amidst hearty cheers. On Monday evening, a tea was given to the children of the parish.*"

ZACHARY PETTITT

Who was this popular benefactor? Zachary Pettitt was born in Great Tey on 27 July, 1838, the third of thirteen children. His father, John, was from a family of farmers, near the Suffolk border. Zachary was said to have come to Paglesham for a weekend to stay with the Wisemans, the oyster merchants, and met his future wife, Alice Anne Browning, whose family had also been in the oyster industry for a least 100 years. Alice was born at Well House, Paglesham in 1845. Her mother, Ann Patience (Coe), whose family lived at Stannetts, sadly died the following year in 1846. In 1862 her father, George Fuller Browning, bought back Cupola House, which had been built by his grandfather Thomas in 1803, and sold in the 1830's. When Alice married Zachary in 1870, they lived at Cupola House until after the death of her father in 1878, when they then moved to the magnificent house of 'Loftmans'. Standing just across the parish boundary in Canewdon, this had been built by Jeremiah Kersteman in 1746, and stood in large grounds with a lake, stables and a coach house where he kept a coach and four. He also farmed West Hall, Paglesham, next door, and with his oyster business as well, remained closely attached to the parish.

He was the largest donor to the major restoration of the church in 1883, and gave both east and west windows. As churchwarden, he was heavily involved with supervising the works, *"as no architect was retained"*.

Zachary and Anne had 9 children, but tragically 5 died while young, probably due to scarlet fever or diphtheria. As mentioned elsewhere, Zachary Pettitt was a great benefactor to Canewdon and, especially, Paglesham, where he was Overseer for forty years. He was a strong Conservative and one of the promoters of the Southend Conservative Club. A mason, he was associated with the Lodge of True Friendship (Rochford).

Zachary Pettitt died on July 8th 1916 and at his funeral the coffin was borne from Loftmans to Paglesham church in a wagon pulled by two horses. His three sons were 'serving with the colours'; Arthur was in France and unable to attend the funeral.

Loftmans, Canewdon - c1929

His daughter Eva had married Percy Hutley in 1903 and they lived at Cupola House until Zachary died, when they moved to Loftmans with their two children, Ted and Margaret (Sue). His widow, Alice, moved back to Cupola House, where she died in 1928. She and Zachary are buried together with their children in Paglesham churchyard, with a low rail round their graves.

A small window, on the south side of the chancel in Paglesham Church, was installed in 1929, in memory of Zachary and Alice, while the west window is dedicated to four of their children who had died by the time of the restoration of the church in 1883.

PAGLESHAM IN THE 1890s

The village in the 1890s was then, as now, physically in two main parts, East End and Church End. The population at the 1891 census showed 270 people in the former, and 207 in the latter, with 13 at Grapnells on Wallasea Island which was then part of the village, giving a total of 490. While Church End and Wallasea men were predominently employed in farming, over half those at East End were in the oyster business. Agriculture was in a major recession nationally, and large areas of the Rochford Hundred had reverted to grass and scrub, but Paglesham's good land had avoided this fate, helped by the prosperity brought by the oyster trade. Of the other jobs, half were in domestic service (mainly females, but including grooms and gardeners). There were also 3 blacksmiths, 2 licenced victuallers and a beer retailer, a coachbuilder, a carpenter, a sawyer, a shoemaker, a grocer and a baker. The Rector, the Rev Thomas Lea, lived in his Rectory (now Ingulfs), and Eliza Hobby was the 'Certificated' schoolmistress living in the school-house.

Only a third of the 105 families in the village had husbands who were born in Paglesham, although another third came from nearby villages. In just eight families were both husband and wife Paglesham-born! But 15 men, like Zachary Pettitt, had married into the village. So this remote corner of the county was remarkably wellknown - and popular!

In 1891 there were 177 children - over a third of the population - under 14, the school leaving age, and by 1899 there were 97 children at the school.

In 1887, Queen Victoria had celebrated her Golden Jubilee and the village, adults and children, had a wonderful day (the first of which we have records) when after a church service they went for a meal in Church Hall Barn where the tables were laden. Ten years later for the Diamond Jubilee, everyone again had a holiday, and after the usual church service, 250 adults and 200 children sat down to a big meal, also in Church Hall Barn, followed by sports and fireworks.

Following the creation of County Councils in 1889, came Parish Councils in 1894. The returning officer received 10 shillings for his duties, but the village was so content that the Chairman, Rev Lea, had to report to the County in March 1899, *"I duly called the Parish Meeting by public notice - only one parishioner attended & no nominations were sent in, hence there could be no election - no one attended either of the Parish Councils during the past year for the simple reason that there was nothing to be done"*! Sixteen years elapsed before a short-lived Parish Council was tried again.

So the end of the nineteenth century appears to have been a reasonably prosperous and happy time in Paglesham, even if life was hard and unsophisticated, as is apparent later.

THE OYSTER MERCHANTS

As oysters were the cause of this prosperity, we will start with the merchants who employed a large proportion of the workers in Paglesham. Zachary Pettitt has already been given pride of place as the giver of the Mission Room to the village.

His fellow churchwarden, and the second largest contributor to the 1883 church restoration funds, was James Foster Turner Wiseman. James inherited his share of the oyster business from his father in 1851, together with Marine Cottage and the fields around East End. He soon enlarged the 'cottage' into 'The Chase' - a substantial house with 9 bedrooms, 1 bathroom, a billiard room etc. Outside, the extensive lawns were enhanced with a fountain and a great variety of trees, the kitchen garden with glasshouses, and the stables with a harness room and coachman's cottage. When his estate was sold in 1903, he owned the land and most of the village at East End, having built 3 rows of cottages. He married Annie Clark and had 8 children. She died in 1889. By then James himself was not well due to diabetes, and gradually his eyesight was going, so he decided to leave Paglesham in the early 1890's. He let his estate to Arthur Nicholls, and sold many of his possessions at the Corn Exchange, Chelmsford, on July 21 & 22, 1891. These included 5000 books, many prints including original Hogarths in complete sets, many valuable paintings by Constable, Van Dyck, Lely etc., and a substantial cellar of wines. James went to live at Plumtree, outside Nottingham,

Particulars.

LOT ONE.

"The Chase," Paglesham.

A VALUABLE COMPACT

Freehold Residential Estate

COMPRISING —

The Residence which contains :—

Dining and Drawing Rooms with bay windows, Entrance Hall, Smoking Room, and Office, Breakfast Room, China Closet, a full-sized Billiard Room with Lavatory, Kitchen, Scullery and Cellar, Nine Bedrooms, Bathroom and w.c., with front and back staircases.

The Outbuildings, &c., include :—

A brick and tiled Brew House, Chaise House, Coal and Knife House, w.c., large Tank (underground) for soft water, with stone cover and a pump of good water, and a back entrance from Causeway leading to Farmery.

The Pleasure Grounds

These are tastefully laid out with shaped flower beds, figure fountain, and an extensive lawn, bordered by a mass of ornamental trees and shrubs, including choice specimens of red and white Cedars, Pines, Firs, Wellingtonias, Variegated Yews and Maples, Walnut, Sycamore, Beech and Laurels, approached by a delightfully cool avenue of Chestnuts and Poplars, the tout ensemble having a most charming effect.

Kitchen Garden and Glass.

There is about an acre of Kitchen Garden, well sheltered and planted with choice fruit trees. The Glass Houses comprise :—Double-span Vinery, 60 feet by 24 feet, in three divisions, with choice heavy bearing vines including Black Hamboro, Muscats, Madisfield Court, Black Alicant, and numerous other sorts. Double-span Peno House with brick bed for Peno 50 feet by 16 feet and divided into two compartments.

These houses are fitted with 4 inch hot-water pipes and valves and Thames Embankment boiler. Brick and slated Furnace House, brick and tiled Tool House, and the brick frames for lights with surrounding forcing pits.

Stables.

On the opposite side of the Causeway leading to Farmery, there is a brick and slated range of Stables with two open stalls and three loose boxes, paved with blue Staffordshire bricks, and having a ventilator in roof. Harness Room and Conchman's Cottage containing five rooms with small Garden.

Nut Ground.

This is nearly 4 acres in extent, and is planted with Kentish Cobs and Filberts, remarkable for their good bearing quality.

The Farmery comprising :—

Brick and tiled Stable with enclosed Shed, Barn, Cowhouse, Poultry House, Open Sheds and Loose Box, the whole surrounding enclosed Yard with high boarded doors. Granary on stone piers, Poultry House and Pond.

Sale of The Chase - 1903

where he married again, and had another son, Sam. He died there in 1903, aged 67, but was buried in Paglesham churchyard, alongside his parents and his first wife. The estate was then sold.

Apart from being an oysterman, he had farmed 700 acres in Great Stambridge and 600 in Paglesham. He was well known in the county, a strong Conservative, and a writer of several books. He also took up painting. He played cricket and was a keen shot, keeping a 'Game Book' of his successes. He spent many winters in Holland, wild fowl shooting.

His knowledge of Essex history, reflected in his library, is epitomised in his 84 page epic poem *'Isoline: A Tale of Hadleigh Castle. 1272'*, which he also illustrated. On more local subjects, his *'A legend of Paglesham'* refers to the hollow 'Smugglers' Elms's, which stood at the Pound Pond until the 1970s, and to his local alehouse.

"...three pollard elms are still standing - when there
Climb up one, and look down its cavernous trunk,
Or descend if a man of good mettle and spunk,
You may - mind I don't say you will - chance to find
Some "Schnapps" or cigars, left by smugglers behind,
If you don't 'tis no matter - Go then without fail
Some half-mile on to the Pub - Plough and Sail,

> At East End you'll find it - When there don't forget,
> Order oysters, bread, butter with stout (heavy wet),
> - As often 'tis called there by both of the sexes -
> 'Tis Courage's brewing, and marked with XXXs;
> When before you   - the stout, bread and butter - they set 'em,
> Then ask for the oysters - I wish you may get 'em!   "

Frederick John Wiseman, a cousin of James F T Wiseman, also inherited oyster layings and the family house. He called it Buckland House, after his great friend, the naturalist and marine biologist, Frank Buckland, who also helped him with diseases in the oysters. His parents and grand parents had lived there - the Victorian part had been added

James Foster Turner Wiseman
(1835 - 1903)
of The Chase

Frederick John Wiseman
(1829 - 1897)
of Buckland House

on in 1854. He married, in 1859, Rosaline Pizzey from Rayleigh, and had 8 children - two of whom died young from scarlet fever. Fred Wiseman was well known in the area both as a staunch Conservative and in the Masonic world. At concerts in the village, and as far afield as Mersea, he would sing and give amusing recitations.

There were normally two live-in servants at Buckland House, a cook and a housemaid, who were paid £2 12 0d each, every three months. In 1887, they frequently handed in their notice, and later withdrew it!. There was also a gardener/groom. Mrs Leavett, of 6, New Row, East End, did sewing, charging 3s for three nightshirts for Arthur.

Their eldest two sons, Frederick William and Arthur, continued in the oyster business and took over from their father when he died in 1897. Arthur married Audrey Leach in 1892 and bought 5 acres of land to build a large house with a live-in servants wing. It was finished in 1899 and called Redcroft. He planted a great variety of trees including a Blue Cedar and a Mulberry. (The collection was doubled to some 50 species in the 1970s and '80s.)

Frederick and Rosaline's third daughter, Mary, (Pet) married Mr Edward Bernard Harris, a London surgeon, in 1894. Their daughter, Zillah, was born in London in 1896, and their son, Athelstan, in 1898. As the last member of the Wiseman family to live in Paglesham, Miss Harris was a well known and respected link with the last century. Apart from preserving the family records, of which there is a remarkable collection of letters, diaries, pictures, account books, and press cuttings, she continued the family traditions by keeping a diary, and writing long letters herself. Extracts from the diaries have been used later.

Also described as 'Oyster Merchant' in the 1891 census was Thomas Quy, whose mother, Charlotte, was yet another cousin of James F T Wiseman. Thomas and Ellen Quy lived with their 12 children at Finches, at Church End. In 1881 he was *"Farmer of 50 acres, employing 4 men"*, but having acquired oyster layings, he clearly thought that Oyster Merchant was the more important style.

Athelstan and Zillah Harris - c1903

THE VILLAGE

We always feel that Paglesham has changed little in the last century, so let us look at what the buildings were like in the 1890s compared with today.

Church End Road

Church End is approached past West Hall and Ingulfs, neither of which have obvious differences externally. Ingulfs had been built as the new Rectory in 1862, and so was only 30 years old when the Mission Room was opened. It is a typically large Victorian house, with high ceilings and extensive outbuildings. It is clear from the speeches at the reopening of the church in 1883, that the Rev Harris found it expensive relative to his means! The earlier 'Parsonage' was on the other side of the road, and had been pulled down when it became uninhabitable. In 1861, it seems to have been lived in by four separate families.

Next, Thomas Quy's house, Finches, looks unchanged although lacking the lime trees once growing close to its frontage. Now known as Finches and Maules, a second and larger house has been added to the rear in keeping with the older part. The field in front is now also kept smartly as the cricket field for the 'Poor Cricketers of Paglesham' team. Last century, cricket was played in afield opposite near the Parsonage, called 'Sweetlips', and in the Bowl field.

Church End

The Punch Bowl, known as The Bowl, used to stand with other cottages on the footpath between the church and school. Between 1838 and 1877 it took over the present building, then called 'Blue House' - because of its colour - which was also said to have been a sail makers. Harvest Suppers and cricket dinners were held there and an annual fair was held in the field opposite.

Two modern cottages precede the 'Punchbowl', while the terrace beyond was completely rebuilt in 1964, although in a modern version of the old style. In 1893, three weatherboarded cottages called Bedford Row stood at the back of the field opposite the 'Bowl'. These only came down in the 1960s. The other houses up to the church were there then, although the brick terrace has had additions made. Next to the Church, Worlds End cottage was an Ale House, run by James Payne, "Beer retailer". Earlier this cottage had been a Dame's School.

The Church (since 1883), and the Georgian Church Hall have not changed at the front. But the farm itself would be

Finches and Maules - c1910

Horse-drawn brakes outside the Punch Bowl - 1900s

almost unrecognisable to the farmworkers of 1893, though the pond might help locate them amid the modern steel and concrete and machinery. The helicopters and crop-spraying aircraft of recent years would have completely amazed them. Beyond the church the five tenements called the Causeway or Winton Haw stood near the pond. Winton Haw is now a large single house built in 1959, set further back.

The Church

Dedicated to St Peter, the church is of Norman origin with much 15th century work. It *"originally consisted of a chancel, nave and tower, which, with the lapse of years, had fallen into a sad and dangerous state of dilapidation"* by the 1880's. Zachary Pettitt and James F T Wiseman, the church wardens, and others raised money by subscription and under their own supervision rebuilt the roof, and added the vestry and south porch. On St Peter's day, June 29th 1883, a grand re-opening ceremony was held.

The Rev Thomas Lea became rector in 1890 and held extra Sunday services, including weekly services at the Mission

Church Hall pond and the church - c1910

Room - to help those who lived 2 miles from the church, in bad weather. He held an Ascension day Communion service in the Mission Room at 4.45 am, so men could be at work by 6 am!

On the last day of the year, the choir were entertained to a supper at Loftmans by invitation of Mr and Mrs Zachary Pettitt. *"During the evening several songs and glees were given by the choir and a few other friends added to the amusement by recitations. After a remarkably pleasant social evening the company joined in singing 'Auld Lang Syne' just as the old year was departing and the new year dawned on happy hearts"*.

At the end of the 1890s Fund Raising was needed again. The organ, was given by a Mr Hargreaves, who had been staying at the Rectory, and it was in urgent need of repair at a cost of nearly £20. The floor of the organ chamber, having decayed, was renewed and ventilators were put in the walls at a considerable additional cost. Proceeds from concerts were £4 12s and £2 9s., the Jubilee collection of 1897 made £2 7s. With other collections and contributions, £32 16 1d was raised.

East End Road

The road to East End has changed considerably. Just beyond Ingulfs, Woolf's Cottage, pulled down in 1959, and the Haunted House are gone. An apiary occupies the site. Claverham Cottage has been converted from a pair of cottages. The old Methodist Chapel, later Congregational, was only demolished in 1992. Its simple rectangular shape was a reminder of older times to the motorist speeding round the bend, though it had been unused since the new chapel was brought from Sutton in 1954, and erected opposite the old school.

The Rev Walter Fuller became Pastor of Paglesham (and Canewdon) in 1893. He celebrated his 7th anniversary in 1900 with a Harvest Festival on the Sunday and on the Wednesday a tea meeting and an evening meeting - *"people filling every available seat"*.

The school was built in 1849 under the auspices of Lady Olivia Bernard Sparrow, who gave the land. She was a noted benefactor, building schools in Leigh and elsewhere. The site would have been chosen as it was between Church End and East End. There were no other houses around it until 1935. East End children, especially the five year olds, had a long walk over the rough roads, full of puddles at times. Their feet were often soaked before they reached the school. For those coming from Church End, the bend in the path took them round the site of the old Punch Bowl.

13

The school was enlarged in 1872 and again extended in 1894, at a cost of £300, to take 120 children. It had a second classroom, with a gallery (taken away in the early 1900's) and washrooms. The greatest number of children the school had was 97 in 1899. By 1910 there were only 70 children and in 1923 numbers dropped to 46. From then on numbers varied between 35 and 50 until the late 1970's when by 1978, it was down to 24. Six years later it closed for good.

The school was always a focal point in the village, especially before the Mission Room was built, as it was the only place where large numbers could gather. Even then, the school was still used for some meetings and entertainments as it was more central for the whole village.

Now the school has been split into two, further extensions made, and two modern houses created. The old washrooms are now part of a garage. The semi-detached houses to the west were built after the Second World War, the Council houses to the east in 1935, commemmorating King George V's Jubilee.

Paglesham School - c1895, by Allison Bond, 1990

Halfway to the turning to East Hall used to stand the old parish workhouse, now gone, as has the old East Hall, damaged by a bomb in 1942. The present house was built in 1964, and the cottages alongside are also post-war. But the brewhouse still survives, together with the old barn, though the old timbers of the latter have been given a new brick base, and it has been extended by steel-framed storage barns. Beyond, both Clements and Clements cottages - a community of 20 people in 1891 - have gone, but Grape Vine Cottages survive, extended and modernised. Round the corner, Well House, where the Brownings had lived, and in 1891 the Popplewells, has little changed, though the trees in its garden suffered badly in the 1987 'hurricane'.

The Riverside

Across the fields to the river, we find a scene very different from 100 years ago. Only the old boatshed, with its piles in the tides, and a small store on staddle stones remain. The oyster industry with its 60 workers has gone, though the pits are still visible. Boatbuilding, its carpenters and blacksmiths, sawpit and smithy, has been reduced to the fitting out of glass-fibre hulls. The imposing timber barges and smacks have been replaced by a shoal of pleasure craft. A second boatshed was built in the 1970s, on the landward side of the sea wall, and the boatyard has expanded and filled with sailing and motor vessels of all sizes.

January of 'Mission Hall year', 1893, started very cold, with heavy snow and freezing temperatures all day. The oystermen had to work hard taking off the ice from the pits so that the oysters didn't die. Over the next few days, the river was almost full of ice.

William Hall was the boat builder until 1895, and he had built Zachary Pettitt's screw driven steam powered dredging boat in 1886, the first steam vessel to be built at Paglesham, which caused a great deal of interest. It was christened 'Tiny Mite' by Zachary's little daughter, Eva Pettitt, aged 3. His successor, James Shuttlewood, took over the boatyard in 1895 and built a 40 ton lighter for carrying purposes - again for Zachary Pettit and this time christened the 'Arthur' by master Arthur Pettitt, Zachary's youngest son.

The highlight of the year for those in the oyster business and spectators were the Regattas. The first was held in 1858 and recorded in 'The Illustrated London News'. As far as we know it was held fairly continuously to the 90's and consisted of a race between the oyster smacks, to Creeksea Ferry and back to Paglesham, twice. In the early 1890's,

Barges on the River Roach - c1910

The timberyard and thatched barn at the boatyard - c1910

Fred Wiseman's 'Secret' and 'Viking' raced Zachary Pettitt's 'Alice' and 'Kate'. The steam launch 'Tiny Mite' carried Zachary Pettitt and friends and followed the race. The 'Secret' won, 3 1/2 minutes in front of the 'Alice'.

That evening, a free dinner was given in a marquee outside the Plough and Sail, paid for by several influential gentleman. *"Previous to this, however, coppers were scrambled for by the children of the parish and races were run by men, boys and girls for money prizes . . . at the conclusion of the repast an adjournment was made to a field where sweets and nuts were distributed to the children."*

The company then returned to the marquee for a *"carnival evening"* under the chairmanship of Mr Pettitt. Speeches were interspersed with musical items and amusing recitations by Mr Fred Wiseman.

The nearly blind James F T Wiseman came in for a little while and was *"accorded with an ovation"*. He told the company he was sad to say he would soon be leaving Paglesham.

At the Rochford Petty Session the previous week, *"Considerable amusement was caused by a publican applying for an extension on the occasion of 'Paglesham Regatta'. The idea of quiet little Paglesham having a 'Regatta' seemed altogether too funny."*

Hallowe'en in the boat shed - 1950, by R S Choppin, 1987

Oyster dredgermen, outside Plough & Sail - early 1900s

Milton Villa, New Row and Shop Row, Waterside Lane - c.1910

East End

Back up the lane to East End, the sewage treatment works are only 25 years old (1968), but the next cottages (one now extended) were there in 1893. Lost in some scrub is the site of Water Rat Hall, William Hall the boatbuilder's home, earlier called Marsh House. All the rest of the houses on that side of the road have been built since the Mission Room. Milton Villa was built by James Shuttlewood in 1899. He had followed William Hall as boatbuilder. On the side was a shop to sell surplus produce from his very large garden, and honey from the bees, while sweets were also sold. The house was later used as two flats, and the outside staircase was only removed in 1993.

James's son, Frank, built Shore Ends in the river end of the garden, and took over the boatbuilding in the early 1930s. Two other houses have been built since the war, in between. At the corner of the lane, Cobblers Row retains the same name as an earlier group of six tenements, pulled down in the 1930s.

With the oyster business thriving, James F T Wiseman built three rows of cottages in 1873, for 20 families. He diverted the road round them so it no longer went through his garden at The Chase. Two of the rows had six cottages each with a wash house, coal house and wc each. In the 1891 census the ones beside the road, New Row, and sometimes known as Brick Row, were called Tailor's Row. Shop Row was Rice's Row - George Rice was Postmaster and his wife, Sarah, kept the shop. Her sausages were famous. Made from pigs kept by the Popplewells at Well House, it is said that 1 cwt a week were sent to Scotland. In 1899, they cost 9d a pound. The shop closed in 1985, and was converted into a house. Boarded Row was called Scandal Row - 8 cottages in all, a wash house each, but only four toilets. While little changed on their fronts, the rear outhouses of Shop and Boarded Rows have been drastically altered to provide more space and indoor 'amenities'. Some houses now take two of the old ones, with rooms combined as well, while solar panels on one cottage would puzzle the Millers, Olleys or Pottons of 1891. One cottage is, however, lived in by the descendants of those living there then. The four cottages of Barn Row, next to the shop, are today a holiday home. 'Swatchways', built in 1966 with its living accommodation upstairs, brings us to the 'Plough and Sail', as popular a venue now as in the last century.

The Plough and Sail

The Plough and Sail, at East End, stands at the end of the road. The wide part outside was called the 'Endway' where Fairs were held. William Staines was the 'Licenced

Victualler' in 1891. Many social gatherings were held in 'the Plough', including Hector Pettitt's Coming-of-Age in 1892, where all the men in the Pettitt oyster business were entertained to a "substantial repast" - "The dinner was served at 5 o'clock, and after the cloth had been removed, refreshments, cigars and tobacco were provided and the time was pleasantly whiled away in a convivial manner. After speeches and toasts and the presentation of a 'handsome marble clock' to Hector, songs were sung by various men - the gathering terminated at 10 with the singing of the National Anthem."

There was a similar event for all the farm workers that worked for his father, and Hector also celebrated with a Ball at the Royal Hotel, Southend. This started at 8.30 pm and continued until between four and five o'clock in the morning. A "recherche supper was served in the coffee room".

The pub's oven could be used by the villagers. After the bread had been baked in the oven, they could bring their joints of meat, pies or other cooking at the cost of 1 penny. This facility continued until well into this century. Nine-pin bowling was played in the pin shed at the rear.

When it was sold, following James F T Wiseman's death in 1903, the lease was held by Messrs Luker and Co, and Alfred

LOT TWO.

The "Plough and Sail" Inn,

FULLY LICENSED.

WITH LARGE VEGETABLE AND FRUIT GARDEN,

POSSESSING :

A Frontage of **97** feet with an open space **19** feet in width from the House to a boundary mark on north side of the main road leading to "THE CHASE," PAGLESHAM, and close to the Entrance Gate.

THE INN contains:

Parlour, Keeping Room, Pantry, Bar, Taproom, Four Bedrooms and Cellar with Bedroom over.

THE OUTBUILDINGS, &c., comprise

Bakehouse with Oven and small Yard, Lean-to Shed, small paved Yard, w.c. brick and tiled Pin Shed, Chaff-house, Stable with two loose boxes, Lofts over Chaise House, two Piggeries, w.c. and Yard.

This Lot (together with the Store House in two floors forming part of Lot 12) is held by Messrs. Luker & Co. under a Lease for 14 years from 29th September, 1898, at the

A charabanc and party outside the Plough & Sail, c.1919

The Chase, from the sale catalogue - 1903

Kemp was publican. He was succeeded by his wife, Nellie, up to 1929. They catered for charabanc trips as it was a popular venue for those who liked oysters. Many people would eat two dozen oysters at 2s 6d a dozen, with brown bread and Guinness.

A Public Bar was added in the 1930s, and the whole renovated in 1968. Further extensions at the back have given more space for the restaurant facilities which are an essential part of pub trade in the 1990s. No longer is the Plough primarily a 'local', although it is still well patronised by local people. The size of its carpark shows that many patrons come from the very large population less than 15 minutes away!

Near the 'Plough'

Chaseway Cottages stand beside the old track to the river. They are some of the oldest in village and have been estimated to be from about 1626. Two modern houses have been built just beyond them, in the 1960s. The Chase has already been described. Although externally still much the same, internally it is two elegant dwellings. Across its farm lane, the horseman's cottage has been increased in size, and the stables converted in 1973 into a small but delightful cottage. James F T Wiseman's farm buildings, which he included in a painting of 1881, still stand beside their pond.

Returning past the 'Plough', Buckland House, the Wiseman family home, has also been mentioned, and is little changed, except that weather boarding has been removed. Buckland Cottages were built by the Wisemans and have MDCCCIL (1849) on them. They stand next door to the Mission Room, with Newlands, built 1957, set behind them.

This completes the nucleus of East End, which despite the alterations and additions, would still be familiar to late Victorians.

Back to East Hall

Continuing along the road towards Rochford, past Zachary Pettitt's Cupola House, with its Georgian frontage unchanged except for its restored windows, the next change would be that the ancient 'Rose Cottage', called Lunts Cottage in 1891, is now the modern 'Hove To', the name given by Walter Keeble when he built a smaller house in 1937. The Keeble family took over the oyster business in the 1920s from Fred and Arthur Wiseman, whose house, Redcroft, is next door.

The Hutley family, a friend and Governess,
outside Cupola House - 1912

Rose Cottage, predecessor to 'Hove To' - c.1910

Further down the road, a new pair of semi-detached houses were built in 1893, by Zachary Pettitt, to go with two pairs his father-in-law, George Fuller Browning, had built in 1876. Four of these six have now been extended from their two-up-two-down origins.

The next bungalow, Glenthorpe, was built by the Shuttlewoods in 1926. Opposite are the old gravel pits, worked up to the 1930s and used to test vehicles in preparation for D-day in 1944.

Where the road turns the corner at South Hall Farm, a pair of 1960s cottages precede farm buildings of which only one is old. Stannetts, down its own lane, may look much the same, but internally a renovation in the 1970s has changed it into a large comfortable home.

Stannetts, by R S Choppin, 1987

OBS Cottages were built in the 1860s by Lady Olivia Bernard Sparrow, who then owned South Hall and East Hall Farms. Both these cottages are twice the size they once were. South Hall, once the name of the demolished manor house at the farm, had been called Paglesham House, and Pound House (after the parish pound beside it). Frederick John Wiseman sold the house in 1898 to Henry Brown, of whom more later.

The original South Hall had been registered as a Quaker place of worship in 1704.

This brings us back to the East Hall road and completes the tour of the village. The feeling of continuity felt today is justified. The changes that have occurred in the last 100 years are relatively small compared with the major similarities with the end of the nineteenth century. Greater change has come about in the people of the village and their lifestyles. Let us look further at life in the 1890s.

VICTORIAN LIFE

Clothes

While many aspects of life 100 years ago provide a contrast with today, some aspects of modern living started surprisingly early.

In 1893 a new way of shopping was being advertised in the Southend Standard. John Noble of Princess Street, Manchester offered "Direct from the manufacturer by means of Parcel Post at less than half the ordinary prices. A perfect Revolution in the cost of garments for ladies - half guinea costumes - knock about frocks from 1s 6d each". Shoes were advertised from Olley at Rayleigh 2s 0d for a pair.

Victorian costume, from a Wiseman scrapbook

Many mothers must have found it hard to dress the children as the families were often large, but the girls always wore a white pinafore on top of their clothes. Boys would have worn white collars to church, and to school. Although it is not often stated, families then would have made use of the technique of 'handing down' clothes from older children to younger, even more than is done today.

However, as a child of a well off family, Edith Hope Dannatt, who was born in 1884 and later married Frank Wiseman, remembered wearing "a vest, calico chemise, stays, white calico draws withfrills of embroidery just below the knee, a red flannel petticoat during the week and white on Sunday, a top petticoat, a frock and a white pinafore, black woollen stockings, a hat with elastic under the chin. I wore black kid button boots, with patent toe caps of which I was very proud, our boots were always made for us."

At the age of 7 she had a mantle instead of a coat. She had her first long dress at 17, two inches above the ground. *"At this age it was considered immodest to show above the ankles"*. Little boys wore frocks, petticoats and buttoned up draws until 4-5 years old.

Mourning was frequently observed, the period of which being governed by the closeness of the relative. For adults, full black was worn - 2 years for a widow and 1 year for a brother and sister. Even children went into mourning. At 10 years old, Edith lost a little brother and wore black for 6 months and then went into half mourning for the next 6 months, wearing black and white or a grey dress. Black was worn for a month when Queen Victoria died in January 1901.

Trips to Southend

The Band of Hope, a temperance organisation, organised a trip to Southend Pier in June 1893 - the new iron pier with its 'toast-rack' electric train, was only four years old then. They would have travelled by horse-drawn brake. *"It took those in charge nearly all their time to look after the children, as they were wild with delight, some of them having never ridden on a train. At about 4 o'clock a tea was provided at the Victorian Coffee Palace - justice was done to all the good things provided. After tea and another stroll on the beach, the return home took place and many thanks were due to the kind friends at Hockley and Ashingdon."*

Edith Hope Wiseman, writing in 1966 of her memories of a holiday in Southend in 1899 said: *"My 'all in one' bathing costume, which buttoned high up under the chin, had sleeves and finished with frills below the knee. I undressed in a bathing machine which was drawn by a horse up and down the 'ladies only' beach so that we descended out of the back door straight into the water. I was reprimanded by the bathing attendant because the top button of my costume was not fastened."*

Travel

Southend, which had become a Borough in 1892, was expanding fast. The Southend Standard in August 1893 mentions that a great number of people came to Southend on Bank Holiday Monday (then the first Monday in August) - there were now two train services for them to arrive by. Excursion tickets cost 5s 0d return 1st class, 2s 6d third.

The Wisemans travelled quite regularly to London - the line from Liverpool Street to Rochford and Southend was opened in 1889. Before this they took their donkey cart to the Gore, or drove to The Kings Head at Rochford, where they boarded the horse drawn bus to Southend, to catch the 'express' train to Fenchurch Street.

The Wiseman and Pettitts used their oyster smacks to travel up the coast to Colchester, Brightlingsea or Mersea, or over to the continent where they regularly traded. James Wiseman spent more than one visit shooting near Ostend, and painted the buildings of an oyster company there. If the destination was inland, say Southminster where among other places Fred went to sing, he would ride, crossing the Crouch on the Creeksea Ferry, or fording it at Hullbridge. Fred also had a donkey cart and a phaeton.

There were 2 public carriers with whom one could get a ride to Rochford with the heavy goods - one at Church End and one at East End. In 1891, Henry Kemp, living at Cupola House, was one. On a Thursday which was market day in Rochford, cattle and sheep being driven along the lanes were a familiar sight.

Roads were very poor - full of ruts and puddles - and especially bad in winter. Everyone walked a great deal, making use of footpaths. Apart from Rochford, Burnham was another place for shopping - especially for leather boots - men walking to Creeksea and taking the ferry.

Farming

In the country life was hard for the farm workers - men and women worked in the fields from dawn to dusk. Their only days off were Sundays, Christmas Day and Good Friday. Zachary Pettitt was very aware of the state of farming due to cheap imports of grain from Canada. At a Smoking Concert at Rochford, in a speech he made in the depressed 1890s, he said, "When he first started farming (c 1870) he was able to pay his men 18s a week. Indeed he had difficulty getting men at that price. Now wages had come down to 14s and loads of men went to him for work. The cheap loaf had been the curse and the bug bear of the farmers. (hear, hear) ....If the farmers could get 50s a quarter for their wheat, then they would be able to pay the old scale of wages." His men appreciated his real concern. In a letter from "The Unemployed of Canewdon" to the local paper - thanking Zachary Pettitt for employing 14 men -

they said, "If it had not been for him we should all now be wanting bread!"

Charlie Bannister of Little Barton Hall, Stambridge, remembers how as a young boy of 8 in the '90s, he rode the horse that pulled the reaper, for which he got 2s 0d a week. The man who sat on the reaper put off the corn in sheaves, which 3 men then tied up and stood in traves or stooks. They worked from 5 am until it was dark. Stone picking and docking were other jobs for a boy.

After the corn had been carted in waggons to the nearby stacks, to be threshed later, the gleaners were allowed into the fields to pick up any ears of corn which were on the ground. Often a mother and her children would do it, and the grain would be fed to their chickens.

A familiar sight on the river were the barges - some carried wheat to the mill, but many carried manure from the horses in London and could be seen returning with a stack of hay or straw on their decks. There were two 'loadings' in Paglesham, at Clements and Church Hall, and three at Stambridge. Each barge was unloaded by men with baskets walking across a 30 ft long plank to the seawall. These men would get about £2 10s per barge, working from 6 am to 4 pm, and it would take a day and a half to unload.

Much of the land next to the rivers was called the marshes - grassland where cattle and sheep grazed. Most farms were 'mixed', that is with both arable land and animals, either a herd of cows, or sheep. Sometimes pigs were kept. Even small farms usually had at least a house-cow.

The crops grown were wheat, which went after threshing to Stambridge Mill to be ground, oats and barley. Potatoes were harvested by the women and by children, who were allowed time off from school.

Recreation

The young people of the large houses had a very social life. In the winter they would go to balls and dances in Southend, sometimes travelling by Lazell's 'close trap' (10s one way!), and arriving home in the early hours. On one occasion they went to Creeksea by horse bus, leaving Buckland House "at 1/4 to 8" in the evening, at a cost of 30s. Even for a group this was an enormous sum.

The Wisemans went over to the Pettitts at Loftmans at times to practice for concerts to be held at the School or the Mission Hall, at which they would play the piano, or sing, or give recitations. Tennis parties in summer and dances in winter, in each others' houses, were all part of their

Confirmation Card for
Ella Mary Woolf, signed by the
Rector, Rev Thomas Lea - 1897

lives, as was Church and a walk on Sundays. Visitors to Buckland House from the Rectory would often be walked home. Such was the walking habit that in her 70s, Miss Harris would still walk back to the Chaseway, at night, if she missed the last bus from Rochford.

The men went to Smoking Concerts, called 'a Smoker', in the Old Ship, at Rochford. They didn't have the same health worries as today. But Dr King charged 1 shilling for a visit to his surgery, or 2s 6d for a home visit, and medicine could be 3s 0d, so the workers would have been keen to stay well. Otherwise home remedies were used.

Cricket was played near the Punch Bowl, or opposite Milton Villa. In hard winters they all went skating - Barton Hall Creek was one venue.

The Rochford Hundred Coursing Club met at Church Hall, where Mr Henry Meeson farmed for about 40 years, and Mrs Meeson after him, and on Zachary Pettitt's land. The Victoria County History states: "Better coursing it would be difficult to find than that obtained over these fields, although the adjacent marshes do not furnish quite such legitimate trials". Now few hares are to be seen, due rather to changed agricultural methods, rather than coursing. Zachary became President of the Club, and "generously offered the whole of his fine estate for coursing purposes."

THE NEW CENTURY

Church

In 1902, the Rector wrote in the Service Book - *"Many families have left the village in the last 2 years and the majority have been church people and communicants"*. The population of the village had dropped by 35 between 1891 and 1901, and continued to fall by about 50 each ten years until 1931.

The Boer War, 1898 - 1902, far away in South Africa, probably had little impact on the village, but on June 8th 1902, there was a Special Service in the church - 'Thanksgiving for Peace'.

In 1902, therewere again *"large village celebrations for the coronation of King Edward VII"*. The ceremony was postponed from June 24th to August 9th, as the King had to have an operation for acute appendicitis. But as the harvest would be in full swing, Paglesham held its festivities earlier. A service was followed by a dinner, where *"eight long tables groaned beneath the weight of good things"*, again in Church Hall barn. Similar celebrations took place only 9 years later, when King George V was crowned.

The Rector's account shows that for the Sunday School Treat in August 1904, there was a great amount of food

Paglesham Church - 1980
by Allison Bond

6 lbs sugar, 3/4 lb tea, 5 1/2 loaves cost 2s 6 1/4d, 28 lbs of cake cost 14s. There were also buns, madeira cake and rice cake.

In 1905, the Rev Thomas Lea died. The text for his last sermon "Dust thou art and into dust shalt thou return" was long remembered for its aptness. His funeral was attended by practically everyone in the village - the women especially being attired in mourning. He was held in the deepest affection by his parishioners, both old and young. Children put primroses, violets and evergreens on his grave. To the church he had given a reredos and a reading desk which he had made himself.

He was followed by the Rev William Fraser and he, his wife and family did much for the village over the next sixteen years.

'Flower and Egg' services were held for many years, starting in 1906. In June 1913, 214 eggs and 80 bunches of flowers were collected and sent to a hospital (usually the London or Shadwell Children's Hospitals).

Mrs Fraser started the Mothers' Union and the Girls' Friendly Society. Girls of fourteen and over would go to the Rectory to have tea and to sew.

Arthur Wiseman, who had been organist since 1890, and a lay reader since 1896, was also Superintendant of the East End Sunday School. School treats appear frequently in the Rector's Service book. Ralph Wiseman, Arthur's son, remembered how, every Sunday whatever the weather, his father rode his bike the 1 1/2 miles to church, walking the last 1/4 mile. He played the organ for the morning service, and returned to Redcroft for lunch. In the afternoon he took the Sunday School at the Mission Room, returned for tea, and then went back to church to play for the 6.30pm evensong.

The Mission Room was used for many years as a Reading Room until long after the Great War. Books could be borrowed, and in the evening there was instruction in reading and writing. Those who used it were so grateful to John Popplewell, who had been its mainstay and helper for a long time, that in 1906 he was presented with an inscribed marble clock (still going nearly 90 years later) for his valuable service.

In 1908 twenty one donors gave trees to beautify the churchyard, most of which, including limes and the oak, still stand today in 1993.

Cycling

At the turn of the century, bicycles were becoming popular - though expensive. Gents cycles were advertised in the Southend Standard on 26 April for £12 12s and Ladies £13 13s - they were mostly used in summer because of poor roads in winter.

The first lady in Paglesham to own a bike was Ella Mary Woolf, in 1905, who lived with her parents at the cottage, later known as Woolf's Cottage, which had a famous vine which made wonderful wine.

In early days of cycling, ladies had to wear special clothes so their legs were not exposed. This consisted of a coat, an ankle length skirt and heavy cloth bloomers which fitted below the knee. The skirt was kept down by a wide elastic band which fitted under the shoe and was pinned to the bottom of the skirt.

Transport

The horse-drawn brakes would bring trippers out to the country. In 1904, the landlady of the Royal Oak, Stambridge, said *"The shameless conduct of those trippers*

'The Trading Post', and Barn Row, East End, 1970s

who periodically made a progress in brakes through this quiet marsh land country - after much horse play in the village filling the air with barbarous dissonance". They may have been on a 'Mystery Tour', for which Paglesham was often the destination, pausing for the reputed haunted house beside Woolf's cottage to be pointed out, and presumably being refreshed at the 'Plough'.

Sometimes a man with a red flag walked in front of a traction engine or the early cars to warn horse-drawn vehicles - so they could move off the road - horses became very frightened of these new contraptions.

Shops

By 1905 Miss Emily E Rice had taken over the shop at East End and her accounts show little change in prices compared with her mother's in 1899. The famous sausages remained 9d per pound, pork was up from 8d to 9d, lard - a popular item was still 8d. Accounts were often only paid annually, which must have been as difficult then as it would be today.

She was also sub-postmistress. Letters arrived from Rochford at 8.30 am and were dispatched at 3.40 pm (2.30pm in 1912), Sundays 10.20 am. The nearest money order office was at Canewdon and the telegraph office at Rochford (6 miles distant). The letter-box was in the window of the shop, and the double-pane that replaced it when it was moved to the Plough could be seen until the shop itself was closed and converted into a house in 1985.

William Atkinson was shopkeeper and churchwarden at Church End, where the famous smuggler 'Hard Apple', William Blyth, had also kept the village shop, in the early 1800's. Blyth was churchwarden too and is said to have used the church registers to wrap up the bacon and butter.

The Atkinson family came to Church End in 1910 from London. William was also a famous violin maker, making his first in 1869 at the age of 18. It was a well-known sight to see his violins drying on the line outside the shop. He married in 1880 and died in 1929. To quote from his obituary, "He claimed to have found the varnish secret of the Cremonese masters. Although he made over 300 violins, violas and 'cellos and though he could make an instrument in a fortnight, the varnishing and drying took nearly 2 years". He died trying to tell his son the composition of the varnish but the secret died with him. His instruments are still highly regarded.

The shop remained in the Atkinson family until 1961, when Jim Cousins took over. It finally closed in 1973.

Atkinsons shop, Church End, 1920

The Great War - Territorials by the River Roach - c1915

Accidents

In 1911 there were two fatal accidents. In February, James Powell, aged 5, was crossing the road from the playing field opposite the school when he was run over by the first car in Paglesham, owned by Mr Brown of Paglesham House. The whole school went to the funeral. At the inquest Mr Brown was asked,

> "What speed were you driving? - Top speed.
> "You would have no difficulty in going at 5 miles per hour with a 16 HP Humber? - No, I can go at walking pace in the town."

A witness said that Jimmy had been chased by another boy through a gap in the hedge. Mr Brown, whose father helped found Westcliff Motor Services in 1913, and who himself became its chairman, was exonerated from all blame. It was suggested that it was dangerous to have a playground on the other side of the road, and that Motor Union notices should be put up either side of the school.

In June, the same year, Henry Barnes, aged 8, was running beside a brake outside the Punch Bowl, shouting for coppers, when he fell under the wheels and was killed.

THE GREAT WAR

Church Services

The Rev Fraser was Rector during World War I when 53 men volunteered from the village, the youngest being Fred Farthing who was only 15. They met in the Mission Room and Mr Meeson saw them go, in several charabancs. Ten of the men did not return. The 'Register of Services' shows several special services during the war, starting on August 2 1914, 2 days before war was declared with 'War Sermons'. Other entries include:

13. 9.1914 Parade of Territorial Cyclists of Essex Company.
31. 1.1915 Early service (3.30 pm) started for Evensong as no lighted windows after hours because of war, by command. Soon blinds were fitted and they went back to 6.30 pm.

In October 1917, service hours altered in case of hostile raids, to 3.15 pm.

20. 5.1916 Clocks advanced an hour according to the new Summertime.
23. 1.1916 Being ready for war (invasion) church bells

18. 6.1916 Memorial service for the sailors lost in the Jutland Naval Battle and for Lord Kitchener who was drowned.
12. 7.1916 Funeral of Zachary Pettitt.
 6. 5 1917 Read the Kings Proclamation about food scarcity.
12. 8.1917 Air raid in Southend.
 3. 2.1918 In a census, population 285 with 83 houses.
19. 5.1918 Big German raid over the parish - the LAST.
11.11.1918 Armistice signed.
17.11.1918 Thanksgiving for Armistice.
 1.12.1918 Very wet - epidemic of influenza.

This so-called 'Spanish flu' hit much of the world - it stayed around for 4 months and was at its worst in November and December when the school was closed for 3 weeks.

Miss Harris's Diaries

Miss Zillah Harris and her mother were living back in Paglesham in 1915, perhaps because it was safer than London. Her father became very ill in 1916 and died on September 6th. They lived at that time in Shop Row, East End, and the track was strewn with straw to muffle the sound of horses' hooves. Athelstan had joined up, and he was wounded in October the same year.

Miss Harris wrote a diary in 1915 and 1916, when she was 19, and again from 1933. This gives an interesting account of the village and the Mission Room, where she attended many activities.

In 1915, she records that the first Regulars, and then Territorials, arrived to take up guard duty at the river, and the men were billetted in the village. The school log book in February also adds that the children were very excited to see 300 soldiers marching by. There were 2 guns and a searchlight at East End, and, in the cricket meadow opposite Milton Villa, there was a listening post.

In the early days of the Great War, three bombs dropped near the school, and a Zeppelin hovered in the neighbourhood causing the villagers to spend most of the night outside. German Gotha planes and Zeppelins were seen at times going towards London, and gunfire could often be heard. P C Brown went round to everyone to say that all lights must be shrouded from 5pm to 6am, until further orders, as aeroplanes were about. One Sunday, 68 wounded soldiers, wearing pale blue suits with red ties, came to have tea on the lawn at The Chase, which later became a military convalescent home, as Col Nicholls (Arthur Nicholls' son) was a doctor.

With so many men away at the War, there was a labour shortage and a byelaw was passed in June 1916 allowing children to work in agriculture.

Otherwise, life appears to have continued for many, much as before. There were jumble sales in the Mission Room, with a cup of tea afterwards. There were whist drives and working parties. Tennis teas were held at Buckland House (one of several houses with tennis courts, others being at Redcroft and Loftmans). The shops at Church End and East End continued, although as the war progressed supplies became scarce. Yet Willans also delivered from Rochford. One could travel to town in Potton's trap. In 1915, a charabanc was meant to run, but did not always arrive. The better-off still had their horses, and traps or carriages, and there were even a few cars to be seen.

However, there must have been a background of worry with so many away fighting. Memorial services were held when the deaths of each of the ten village men became known. A memorial in the church for all those who went, as well as the fallen, was unveiled by Col Smeaton on March 23rd 1919.

Zillah, Athelstan and their mother later moved to the Chaseway, and Athelstan went to Australia for several years. Miss Harris ran the library from her front room for 40 years, beginning in the early 1930s and only closing in 1973, when a mobile library took over. She became a keen member of the WI and had a wide range of interests.

Mrs Harris died in 1959, aged 89 and Athelstan, who had been the organist at the church, in 1968. Zillah died in 1979.

BETWEEN THE WARS

Oysters

Kelly's Directory for 1912 says that "*the oyster fishery has of late greatly diminished*". The owners were still Zachary Pettitt, Arthur M Nicholls and Frederick and Arthur Wiseman. It continued to drop off during the First World War and then in 1921 there was a 'death' in the oysters and nobody knew why. Fred and Arthur Wiseman sold the family homes, Buckland House and Redcroft in 1926, the latter for £1800.

Arthur Wiseman, among his other activities, was a school manager and at a farewell presentation at the school, he was given a handsome walking stick and an illuminated address, worked by Lilian Groves and Hilda Shuttlewood.

In 1933, Walter Keeble (who had run the Punch Bowl previously, and who died in 1950) and later his sons, Hubert and Alf, and Hubert's son Ralph, continued the oyster business, but by 1970 they had suffered five set backs - hard winters with frost destroyed much of the spat (the young oyster) in 1939/40, 1947 and 1963. The East coast floods in 1953 swept mud over the oyster beds suffocating both the young and full grown oysters. This happened again in 1958 following a severe electrical storm.

To complete the story, the Keebles finished working in the 1970s. A decade later, unsuccessful attempts were made to restart the industry and a washing plant (a modern requirement) was installed in one end of the boat house. About that time the Rochford District Council promoted a Paglesham Oyster Festival. While not as impressive as the Victorian regattas, a ceremonial dredge of oysters was made and music played by a German brass band from Rochford's 'twin town', Haltern.

A Change of Rector

On the 27 November 1921 at 6.30 pm there was a full church, as it was the last service by the Rev Fraser. On the Friday before, *"The Schoolroom which had been tastefully arranged by Miss Peacock, the school mistress, for the purpose of making a presentation to the Rev William Fraser, Mrs Fraser and Miss Fraser who were leaving the parish amidst many feelings of regret from the parishioners after sixteen years work there."*

In 1922 The Rev C B Jennings arrived, with his wife, 2 sons and 2 daughters. They lived at the Rectory - the last Rector to do so. When they left in 1946, it was sold. Rev Jennings was a familiar sight on his bicycle, and they also had a donkey and cart. He also kept up the tradition of Sunday School outings; that in 1926 was by Motor Bus and cost £1 2 0d plus the tea, £1 0 4d.

In 1926, the Benefices of Canewdon and Paglesham were united by Order in Council, but it was not until Mr Jennings retired that the Rector was shared.

No10 bus - 1920s by Allison Bond, 1993

The Paglesham Bus

Westcliff Motor Services ran a bus service to the village from the 1920s. Operating every two hours between Victoria Circus and the Plough and Sail, the fare was 1s 6d. Stan Galpin who was on the run between 1925 and 1939, recalled that there was no windscreen wiper, so he rubbed a cut potato on the screen to make it greasy and shed the rain.

Women's Institute

The first meeting of the Paglesham WI was held at the school on Friday March 24th 1933, when the county chairman, and county secretary, came. After speeches, a committee of 8 was formed, with Mrs Anfilogoff, of Redcroft, as the first president. Then came refreshments, followed by a rummage sale - to raise money, which was badly needed. The first membership cards included the WI rules. Miss Harris, of course, kept hers and it states:-

> "The main purpose of the Institute is to improve and develop conditions of rural life by providing a centre for educational and social intercourse and activities."

A WI Fete at Redcroft - 1933

Paglesham Women's Institute

A FÊTE AND SALE OF WORK

WILL BE HELD IN THE

Grounds of "Redcroft"
ON
Saturday, July 29th, 1933

To be opened by Mrs. PERCY HUTLEY at 3.30 p.m.
Supported by the Presidents of the various Institutes in the Mayflower Group

DANCES BY THE PUPILS OF MISS BETTY COLLINS
DISPLAY AND GYMKANA BY THE THUNDERSLEY
RIDING SCHOOL (Capt. BARTON)

ADMISSION:
Up to 6 p.m. 6d.   After 6 p.m. 3d.   Children 1d.

Buses leave Southend at 2.45.   Rochford 3 o'clock

Printed by J. Webster Year. Westcliff-on-Sea

Poster for WI Fete - 1933

Membership was only open to women and girls, and the annual subscription was 2s, which could be paid in 2 installments, an indication both of the value of a shilling in those days, and of the hardness of the times. The sub went up to 2s 6d in 1944, and to 50p (10s in old money, the change of currency still causing confusion) in 1972 and £1 in 1974, when the tea cost 4p. In 1993, the sub is £10.50p.

At the beginning - as often since - money was badly needed, so in July 1933, a fete and sale of work was held at Redcroft. Standing in, Miss Tawke opened it, supported by several Mayflower Group presidents, who each received a bouquet. There was a marquee on the lawn, with various stalls, a fortune teller, a dancing display, two horseriding performances by the Thundersley Riding School, and a play. The fete realised £48, a good sum of money in those days.

Social time was very popular, and the ladies took a lot of trouble in entertaining with sketches, charades and monologues. *"A display of physical exercises was given by three members"* is minuted! Various games and singing were also enjoyed. Wouldn't we have liked to be there when Mrs Ducker and Mrs Ellis, dressed in pinafores and bonnets, sang *'You shouldn't play in my back yard'* and on another occasion, when they sang *'Lily of Laguna'*.

Outings were well supported for many years, though to us they might seem like marathons! For example, in 1934, Brighton was the destination. They travelled by Multiways coaches, at a cost of 7s 1d, but 7d was returned in Brighton. During the previous night, heavy storms had caused flooding at the Kursaal and in shops around, but the outing left as planned at 7am, going via the Blackwall Tunnel, and arriving at Brighton about noon. Dinner was 2s, and after a look round the shops, they went to the Aquarium, which cost 6d, where they also had tea (1s). As it was pouring with rain, they went back to the coach early, and left Brighton at 6, getting home about 11, after 2 stops.

The Mission Room

The Mission Room was to become the home of Paglesham WI for the next 60 years. At the time the WI was formed, it was often known as the Club Room, as a Men's Club met there every week. The Men's Club had started in the 1920s, with billiards, darts, card-games and outings, and continued until after the war. By all accounts, the WI was initially not at all welcome!

The Mission Room was then rather different from the cosy room of today. It had a wooden plank floor, and the stage had a little cubby-hole off it for storage. Heating was by a large round stove, opposite the door. The stove was lit by a caretaker, and for many years, a caretaker cleaned the room and put out the chairs in rows. In the early days, coffee was brought by two ladies carrying it on their bikes, one from Church End. Later a Valor heater - one of the tall tubular ones - was used to put a kettle on for tea. In World War II, everyone was asked to bring 2 teaspoonsful of tea - possibly to last for more than one meeting, or it would have made very strong tea!

THE 1930s

When our Women's Institute began, the country was still in the depression, although in Paglesham there was little unemployment. Most of the men worked on the farms, and some of the women as well, doing seasonal work, while other women were 'in service'.

The village had a population of about 310, with 40 or so children at the school. There was no electricity, no main water supply, no sewerage, and very few telephones. In 1934 there was a draught and a new water pump was installed at East End, in Waterside Lane, which was unlocked twice a day. Alfred Kemp rationed out 2 buckets a day, to ensure that the water wasn't wasted. There was a shop at East End, and another at Church End, and deliveries of meat and bread were made from Rochford. Milk in a churnwas brought round from South Hall Dairy on a tricycle , and was ladled out into your own jug.

Miss Harris's diaries provide a view of the times:

May 12 1934 - Rook Shooting - first of season

There was a very large rookery at The Chase and around the buildings beyond.

Alan Boardman on a Fordson, Mission Room behind - c1938

Fred Kemp and Ted May
near New Cottages - 1930s

Milk deliveries
by Tom Wood - 1930s

June 30 - Fete at Redcroft for the WI with a marquee, household stalls, riding, dancing displays etc and on August 1st there was a WI Garden Party there - with a talk on 'Care of the Feet' given by Miss Bowen of Jennings Shoe Shop. A 'Miss Lovely' gave several recitations. There was also a Treasure Hunt and Musical Chairs.'

Even though there was rain in Mid July, the drought was still bad and on

August 11th - The pump at Buckland House is practically dry - only 2ft of water in it, so they are digging a new well on the little lawn having had a water diviner to locate water.

Listening to new Wireless Station at Droitwich, but not sure if our coil is right.

In 1925 the Harris's had paid Mr W C Allen £3 11 6d for their first wireless. This was run by accumulators, which had to be charged regularly.

October 16 - Alfred Kemp attended Nicholls & Smith Bros of Burnham oyster case in London.

October 22 - Col Nicholls won the case. His damages were £2175.

November 2 - Meeting in Mission Room to discuss problems of how we are to all empty our wc's now that the Col Nicholls has given up doing it. Mr Martin was there and it will be done for us, but each house will pay about 6s.

School managers were told that the school may not be used for entertainments unless licensed.

May 6th 1935 was King George V's Silver Jubilee. Nearly every house flew a flag. Celebrations were held in the Bowl meadow, with an outdoor thanksgiving service at 2.15pm, sports, tea for adults and children, more sports and then entertainments. Mrs Meeson presented mugs to the children and they performed, dressed in costume. After a conjuring display and dancing, a chain of bonfires was lit with Paglesham the last, after the glow from Canewdon could be seen. The King spoke on radio in the evening.

May 17th - very hard frost, ice as thick as a penny. Did serious damage all over England. Tremendous damage to potatoes, fruit etc such a frost unknown in living memory.

> June 16th - 50th Anniversary of Mr Jennings ordination and we heard as he preached a touching sermon and hardly anyone could sing the following hymn.
>
> Went down waterside and round wall and back. The wall sides dotted with courting couples - early closing day!

The seawalls were a popular courting place with couples cycling out from Rochford and Southend - often having a drink at the Plough & Sail. Other items included:

> Walked round Bowl meadow - hundreds of rabbits everywhere.
> Beside Clements Farm, filled a carrier bag with mushrooms.
> New violet alter frontal to be finished for next Sunday the 1st in Advent.

In 1936, the death of King George V was duly recorded, "The Kings Life is moving peacefully towards its end", as was the national crisis caused by Mrs Simpson and the abdication of King Edward VIII. Local events sometimes reflected this:

> January 28 - A memorial service at Paglesham church at 4 pm with a good congregation - 4 hymns, including the King's (George V's) favourite, Abide with me.
>
> February 12 - Conservative meeting at 'The Chase'. Mrs Dixon drew a very dismal picture of possible war, how aeroplanes could bomb all ships (food) so no boats, lorries etc could run. Possible treaty between Germany, Italy and Japan. 17 present.
>
> A pair of otters have been heard splashing in water on the marshes.

April 4 - Granny Fletcher 98 today. (She lived to be 105.)

August 22 - Yacht race at Waterside at 4.30 - 13 entries.

November 5 - James Shuttlewood died suddenly.

His son, Frank, continued with the boat building business until Norris's took over in 1960.

> December 7 - Wanted to listen to Baldwin's statement about the King to Parliament in news, but accumulator had run out during afternoon.
>
> December 10 - Went to Buckland House but no WI committee meeting as Mrs Anfilagoff is ill, we adjourned to

dining room for announcement by Mr Baldwin re King
Edward. He has abdicated.

1937 March 8 - (a meeting at the school) to elect 5 on to
the Parish Council which we are having for the
first time

In fact there had briefly been two before. The following
week, there was another meeting to agree to have a Parish
Council, but the motion was defeated 17 to 11!

After the death of Percy Hutley, who had married Zachary
Pettitt's daughter Eva, the contents of his home, Cupola
House, were sold on 15 April. Soon afterwards, Mr and Mrs
Alan Boardman went to live there with their young baby,
Rosemary. He farmed Lunts Farm which went with Cupola
House. (It was sold by the Hutleys in 1973, and eventually
bought by Mr and Mrs Jeremy Zabell in 1976.)

May 12 - kept close to the loudspeaker for the Coronation
ceremony...The service was impressive. Weather
kept fine until 3pm - here terrible rain. service
in the church & tea in Church Hall barn. There
were items by the schoolchildren, a fancy dress
parade, entertainments by Mr Martin's people etc.
Home in time for Empire Broadcast & speech by King
at 8pm.

1938 March 13 - Tide broke through Black Hedge Point, &
near Stannetts Creek stile. Marshes flooded from
High Stile onwards.

March 14 - Walked along seawall to see the breach which is
being repaired by 10 men with sandbags & a palisade
of stakes. It was high tide but didn't go over.

May - ARP (Air Raid Precaution) Committee Meeting - and 14
volunteers for First Aid Classes.

June 24 - Walked to school to ARP meeting at 7.30. Saw
pictures of mustard gas & blisters, also first aid
for gas.

August 1 - Discussions about who Mission Room belongs to.
Rev Mr Jennings did not know, & Diocesan Register
cannot trace it.

September 16 - Mr Chamberlain had a talk with Hitler which
will be continued next week.

This shadow of coming events, which were to change life
permanently, is a suitable point to change the focus of our
review of the last hundred years back to the **Mission Room**.

PART 2

THE WAR YEARS

1939

In 1939, as the country was waiting with apprehension for the outcome of Chamberlain's meeting with Hitler, Paglesham was dealing with its own crisis. The beloved Mission Room was being attacked in order to install electricity, however, WI meetings continued. At the January meeting, which was in the evening at 7.30 pm, there was a talk on cookery and Mrs Phyllis Boardman and Mrs Flo Wood were welcomed as new Members. At the birthday meeting in March, the hall was decorated with paper chains and flags and the news had reached Paglesham that refuse collections were to start in April.

To the June meeting, the hall welcomed nobility in the person of the Marquis D'Oisy, who spoke on 'The story of an old house'. During August, the world situation was reaching boiling point. President Roosevelt had sent appeals for peace to Hilter, to the Polish President and to the King of Italy. All schools were practising evacuation procedures and Mrs Perry was put in charge of a First Aid meeting in the hall.

The first three days of September saw a turning point for the world and for Paglesham. On September 1st, Germany declared War on Poland and the village was told to expect evacuees. On September 3rd at 11am, war was declared against Germany and a party of school children from Chase Lane School in Chingford was despatched to Paglesham.

The WI meeting at the Mission Room was cancelled and preparations were made to receive 33 children and three teachers. Paglesham was sharing in the War effort. Miss Zillah Harris, who in those days spent much of her time cleaning the hall for WI meetings, had two of the children to stay with her, her mother and her brother Athelstan. In her diaries she mentioned the fact that, not only did she have to get the room ready, but also take care of the children. She obviously enjoyed every minute, and Christmas Day with the children in the house was very different from previous years. There were more presents, games including charades and much hilarity; that is until the children went to bed at 8pm with no talking after 9.25pm.

46

1939 also saw a wonderfully happy day for Lol and Gwen Bradley who married, and had their wedding reception in the hall, the catering being undertaken by Garons of Southend.

1940

January 1940 brought rationing of butter, margarine and bacon, but the good news of a son born to Dick and Kathy Thorogood helped brighten the village at that time. The evacuees were taking up a lot of time, but WI meetings in the hall continued monthly.

Lol Bradley and Gwen Wood held their reception at the Mission Room - 1939

2nd World War - Home Guard

Rear L-R: Vin Wood, Jim Thorogood, George Fletcher, Lol Bradley, Arthur Sharp, Bill Fance. Front: Benny Sharp, Tom Keeble, Tom Hines, George Kemp, John Killick, Vic Cardy.

Practical things, like making rugs from old string and undies, were often the topic of the meetings. May saw the closing of Rochford senior school, so the children remained at Paglesham school until they reached the age of 14 years. June saw the return of the evacuees to their own homes as life in Paglesham was becoming quite dangerous. Most nights were disrupted by planes, air raid warnings and incendiary bombs dropping, and there was the added danger of live and dead ammunition being scattered over the countryside. Despite this, life went on.

In September, the Mission Room fence was mended and Paglesham, as aware as always of the plight of others, offered hospitality for bomb victims. The village children had a perilous journey to and from school and often had to dive for cover in the ditches on hearing the planes. Near East Hall, half way to the school, a shelter was built in a ditch, so that they could hide there if caught en route.

Even WI meetings in the hall were disturbed by sirens, as recorded in October, but much more serious problems were arising. The Rev Jennings, who then owned the Mission Room on behalf of the church, had decided to give up or sell the hall. A crisis meeting, which lasted an hour, was called in November but the problem remained unsolved. While decisions were made, meetings continued in the hall and despite the fact that a bomb was dropped on the mud flats, Paglesham was getting down to the serious things in life like a whist drive, held in the Mission Room in December, in aid of the Red Cross.

Miss Harris noted in her diary that *"Jerries were about all evening"*, during the play, but it is doubtful if any of the whist players were disturbed, for the whist players of Paglesham let nothing interfere with their game!

1941

January of 1941 brought an offer of help to use the Congregational Chapel, rent free, for village meetings. The Chapel expected a simple donation to funds, but apparently no-one took up the offer.

February brought more incendiaries to Paglesham but fortunately no-one was injured. The WI met monthly, sometimes in the afternoon and sometimes in the evening, and also an occasional whist drive was held in the hall. May brought great excitement when a plane came down at East Hall, near Harold Brown, who thought at first that the occupants were German, but later on decided that they were English. However, great sadness came to the village when Ernie Cardy was killed by a bomb, while ploughing behind

Church Hall. Many villagers participated in the Home Guard in those days and Mr Loader, who was the Air Raid Warden, would blow a whistle when an air raid was about to happen.

1942

WI Members were still the main users of the hall, but Miss Harris records that Miss Kathleen Jennings, daughter of the Rector, sold National Savings Stamps in the Mission Room each week, raising money for the war effort, although the children had been saving at school since 1940. For its efforts, the village won National Savings Awards which still hang, framed, in the room.

1943

The January WI meeting in the hall took place despite snow and rain. Father Christmas, in the person of Mrs Martin, was a great success. The Rochford Drama Group performed in April, despite having to walk all the way because of three trees that had been blown down on the road in a storm. Shades of things to come?

June meetings of the WI were usually held in one of the members' gardens. However, in 1943 there was a cold wind and showers and the Mission Room hosted the meeting, but the members stretched their legs in Cupola House garden after tea.

1944

1944 found Paglesham, and the WI in particular, addressing very real problems of the world. For the talk in April was on venereal disease. Horizons extended further in May, when the WI had a talk on New Zealand. However, life went on in its everyday way for village people. It was noted in Miss Harris's diary for May, that Rosemary Boardman started school near Chalkwell Park and one can imagine how important that day was for her.

Hitler was still doing his best to disturb village life when a flying bomb caused damage to several windows at Stannetts. There was great excitement and numerous villagers visited to inspect.

Towards the end of the war, Mr A D 'Rawty' Martin gave his farms of Church Hall and East Hall, some 1000 acres worth £60,000, to the nation. He wanted the land to be used as an Agricultural Training Centre for ex-servicemen and women. This never happened, but the National Vegetable Research Station used 150 acres at East Hall for trial plots, particularly for brassicas, for over 30 years.

1945

Despite the war, the January meeting of the WI in the Mission Room was celebrated royally. A Christmas tree was decorated with presents for everyone and the fare consisted of trifle, blancmange, tarts, biscuits, sandwiches and sausage rolls. Games were played which included hide and seek.

A dress parade of fashions of the previous century was arranged by the WI for March to help cheer everyone. Rehearsals were held in the Mission Room and Mrs Eileen Keeble was recorded as helping to get the hall ready, a task she has done on many occasions since. There were 15 people in the parade and Rosemary Boardman presented posies to all the participants. Visitors came from Barling, Little Wakering, Stambridge and they much appreciated the fun. The following Monday, photographs of the Parade were taken for the Southend Standard.

Paglesham had another drama unfold in the middle of March, when an unexploded bomb fell at Stannetts and the school was closed, the children being sent home for safety. To the children's delight, the school remained closed for a month.

March 18th saw a church service held in the Mission Room, as had been the case in earlier times. They are again being held these days. Undoubtedly, the old hall appreciated the singing as it does now.

Accompaniment to singing was once on a harmonium, but this suffered from the effects of damp and mice. Over the years, a number of pianos have come and gone, removed when the WI found it difficult to tell if it was Jerusalem that was being played! Today a small electric organ is brought in for church services. The WI and 'Jerusalem' need no accompaniment!

At the April meeting of the WI the much awaited report from the 'Standard', with photographs of the ladies in their costumes, was read out. The photographs could be ordered at 1/3d each. The talk that they had that day was on Basket Making.

In 1945 also, the WI were a little concerned as mice were beginning to attack the curtains. Today they only attack the cupboards!

In the outside world, Roosevelt died on April 13th, on the 27th Mussolini was arrested, on the 28th Himmler unconditionally surrendered and on the 29th Mussolini was executed.

On May 2nd, as Hitler died in a bunker in Berlin, Miss Harris arranged the chairs at the Mission Room for the following day's WI meeting. The next day brought Miss Bright singing her songs, as the committee could not find a speaker. While this was all going on, the Germans unconditionally surrendered in Italy. May 8th brought the victory (in Europe) announcement and the world and Paglesham could rest again. It had been an eventful few weeks!

Miss Harris, who had been taking care of the hall for the WI until December, now handed over to Mrs Lapwood and against former practice surplus cakes were sold after the WI meetings to augment funds. This is a practice carried on today and many families are thus allowed to share in the renowned delicacies.

POST WAR CHANGES

1946

In 1946, the WI continued to meet monthly in the hall. However, on March 27th a public meeting was called by Mr Alan Boardman and a decision was made to form the Paglesham Village Produce Association (VPA), which was to become another regular user of the Mission Room. Its purpose was to encourage local people to grow their own food in those difficult days. 21 people turned up for this meeting. After a general discussion, films on 'Tomato growing outdoors', 'The Oxford VPA' and 'The siege of Tobruk' were shown.

Following this a formation meeting on April 6th voted in Mr Boardman as the Chairman and Mr Athelstan Harris as secretary. There were 33 members and they decided that the annual subscriptions would be 1s 6d for each family. A committee would be made up of four from East End and four from Church End and notices for meetings would be placed on three notice boards. Meetings would be held monthly and would consist of talks, films and lantern slides. Plants, etc. would be bought in bulk and distributed to members on payment. That first year, 500 tomato plants were sold. Due to late working on the farms, where most of the men worked, there were no meetings in July, August and September. A poultry club was also formed as an associate of the VPA, as at this time many members kept chickens to help out the post-war rationing. This club was run for a number of years, with Dick Thorogood as Chairman.

To achieve its purpose, a spirit of competition was brought into the VPA, and the first VPA 'Produce and Flower Show'

PAGLESHAM
VILLAGE PRODUCE ASSOCIATION
(Chairman - - Mr. A. H. Boardman)

Cover of VPA Programme and Schedule, with Rules. Second Show - 1947

PROGRAMME AND SCHEDULE
OF
PRODUCE & FLOWER

TO BE HELD IN THE

MISSION ROOM
(EAST END)

SATURDAY, 26th JULY, 1947
5 — 8.30 p.m.

OPEN TO THE GENERAL PUBLIC

Classes for

Non-Residents — VPA's — & Kindred Associations

Show Chairman	- - -	Mr. G. KEMP.
Hon. Secretary	- - -	Mr. B. HARRIS.

Committee :
Messrs. W. Bowen, L. Bradley, G. Fletcher, H. Keeble, J. Thorogood and W. Wood.

See Rules on Back

ADMISSION BY PROGRAMME - - 6d. each

Children — 3d. each

WI Ration Book for Mission Room - 1940 -1942

FOOD CONTROL (NATIONAL RATIONING)

8.5

Name and Address of Establishment: *Paglesham Womens Institute, Mission Room, East End, Paglesham, Rochford, Essex*

OFFICIAL ORDER BOOK
FOR
SUGAR

Note.—This book must be used when ordering sugar.

All orders must be numbered in duplicate by the person placing the order.

Catering Establishments and Institutions can only purchase Sugar by filling up and presenting to their retailer a page from this Order Book. A copy of every order must be kept on a duplicate page of the book. Orders in respect of sugar will only be honoured by the retailer with whom the Preliminary Demand Note (S.4) has been lodged. The Order Book, with duplicates duly made up, must be open for inspection by any person duly authorised by the Food Control Committee or the responsible Minister.

Any person knowingly or recklessly making a false statement in respect of any matter specified in this Order Book is liable to a penalty.

was held on 24 August, in the Mission Room. One can imagine the excitement that day brought, as it does to this day, the exhibitors carrying the precious specimens from their many months of toiling, each hoping to walk off with that 'special prize'. At the first show there were 37 classes and 3 for children - a little different to 1993, when there are 125 for adults and 30 for children. However, there has remained no difference at all in the loving care each exhibit is given.

1947

Each year there was, and is, an Annual General Meeting of the VPA, held at the Mission Room. The first in April 1947 showed a balance of £10 13 6d. It was decided that for the annual show for the next year, that is 1948, a marquee would be hired at the princely cost of £2 10 0d., with 30s for transport. It took some time for the VPA to open its committee to lady members and the first two were elected in 1947, one of them being Mrs Ethel Ducker.

About this time Mr Boardman introduced one of the first combine harvesters to the area. This was an Allis Chalmers with a five foot cutting width. Instead of dropping the sheaves of corn, as had the reaper-binder it replaced, it threshed the grain as it went. However, a man still stood on a platform at the side and bagged up the grain and tailcorn. The latest combines, nearly 50 years later, have a 25 foot cut, store up to 6 tons of grain, and will pump this into a trailer alongside, while still cutting new corn.

The WI was still flourishing, holding meetings at the hall and in 1947 they also held a jumble sale and a Christmas bazaar. They forged links at this time with Australia, New Zealand and Southern Rhodesia. The Institutes from these countries sent food parcels to Paglesham and in return the Paglesham Institute sent them books.

A Sunday School was held in the Mission Room in the 1940s, run by Mr Duncan McBriar, the well-known saddlemaker of West Street, Rochford, and his son Alec.

Essex Education Authority started a long battle with Paglesham when it threatened to close the school as there were only 40 children there at that time! Meetings were organised and money raised for a fund to save the school. Mrs Barbara Rampling was put in charge. School numbers grew, as had been predicted, and the school was saved.

Nationally, everyone was celebrating the marriage of Princess Elizabeth to Prince Philip, and Paglesham, despite her worries, celebrated too, by crowding into Mr Watkin's house at East End to watch the wedding on the first television to arrive in the village.

1948

The Mission Room was given a good spring clean in March 1948, and new pink curtains were made by Mrs Joy Lucking, the WI president. Mrs Killick, who went on to play many roles in the WI, was welcomed as a new member this year. Aware, as always, of neighbouring areas, Paglesham sent greetings to the newly formed Foulness Institute. At the August meeting, the competition was a fruit cake and the winner was Mrs Ethel Ducker. Over the years, she has repeated this winning streak with great regularity. She has delighted many a taste bud with her Dundee cakes, wedding cakes, silver wedding cakes, christening cakes and WI birthday cakes. To this day, at 86, she is still giving the WI pleasure with her cooking, although she is a little less nimble than then when she won the musical chairs competition at the June 1948 meeting!

The VPA continued its meetings in the hall during 1948 but had low attendances, some 10 to 14 out of a membership of 54. Discussions took place as to whether to disband, but Mrs Barbara Rampling's encouraging speech carried the day and the VPA continued. Meetings included talks on 'Bees', and 'Soft fruits' and several film shows. One talk of great interest, was when a Mr Ellis came and described the laying of the roof garden at Selfridges. He said that it included two acres of roof space, half of the building acreage, and he had needed two dozen tons of soil to give nine inches for the growing plants. This had to be carried 120 feet above the street level. He also had greenhouses erected, heated by electricity for the raising of the plants. Everyone enjoyed the meeting at which it was noted that 24 members were present, with Mr Ken Rampling in the chair. The 'Annual Show' of 1948 was held for the first time in a marquee, in the paddock at Cupola House, and was recorded as a great success.

On June 12th 1948, The Chase, its farm and 26 cottages - James F T Wiseman's original estate - were sold by auction. The Chase had been made into a 'Residential Hotel or Country Club' after the end of the war, but that did not continue for long. Soon after the sale, it again became a private house, later divided into two, and then three. It has recently reverted to two spacious dwellings.

1949

In 1949 the hall was as busy as usual. The WI meetings saw a talk on 'Road Safety', despite the fact that Paglesham was then a much different village as far as road traffic was concerned, than it is today. However, one thing that has not changed was the fact that no-one at this time wished to accept the post of secretary of the WI and much persuasion had to be brought to bear.

The VPA continued with a talk on pruning in January. A smaller committee for the show was proposed, as it was felt that much valuable time was wasted by irrelevant talk and conversation that cropped up with a larger body, instead of getting on with the job in hand - what words of wisdom! However, it would not be Paglesham without the conversational diversions. There has been many an interesting aside during meetings of the VPA and WI over the years!

At that time, as again in recent years, there was a separate show committee with a secretary in charge. Mr Jim Thorogood, who gave so much of his time over the years to the VPA, was the secretary during those first years. The show committee did not necessarily include only VPA officers. This committee felt that the show in 1949 would be much better off for cash, as *"the balance was to start at £50, so they could afford to splash out a bit"*. How things have changed, we now need something in the region of £300 to run the show, without paying for a marquee.

When the AGM of the VPA changed from April to September in 1949, it became the occasion when cups and medals were presented to show winners. That year, the AGM started behind time due to the late arrival of the bus - another reminder of how times change, as we now have no buses, although we do have a good, subsidised taxi service. The names of the winners were engraved on the cups in those days and each had a certificate to keep. In December, the first annual supper was held in the Plough and Sail and there were 50 people, 35 members and 15 guests. Mr & Mrs Tom Loader were 'Mine Hosts' at the Plough and Sail and given great praise for the supper of steak and kidney and oysters - a feast to repeated many times over the following years.

THE FIFTIES

1950

The WI appreciated a musical programme at the January meeting in 1950. In February, the speaker did not turn up, a familiar problem over the years, so the WI turned to and held a whist drive, which obviously gave them great pleasure. At a talk on birds in March, the lantern did not work properly at first, so there was a late finish! One or two members were worried as they had to pick up children.

These days, we have no young mothers at the WI afternoon meetings. However, recently Miss Valerie Thompson has formed a new evening WI allied to the afternoon group and it has been received with great enthusiasm from mothers and working ladies.

In 1950, some WI meetings were held in the evening like the one in April when 'Trade Balance and Payments' were discussed, a very serious subject. As mentioned previously, each year one of the summer meetings of the WI was, and still is, held in a village garden and this makes such a lovely setting. Sister WI's from the surrounding villages are invited, much to their delight, for many people will come miles for a taste of a Paglesham tea. At the garden meeting in 1950, held in Mrs Lucking's garden, there was a special talk on 'The United States of America'.

"A good time was had by all" at the WI's October evening meeting, which was little wonder, considering that they feasted on tongue salad and cheese, biscuits, sandwiches, ice-cream and coffee and finished with a rendering of Auld Lang Syne (as has continued at Harvest Suppers since). At November's AGM, everyone had a taste of Mr & Mrs Ducker's silver wedding cake. In December, there was a bad fog and members were encouraged to go home early on the school bus - but not before the rendering of carols.

The VPA continued to thrive and hold monthly meetings during 1950. There were interesting debating evenings when subjects included: 'Women should not wear trousers','Summer time is an advantage' and 'The present road safety campaign is inadequate'. One can imagine the heated exchanges as these topics are very relevant today as well as in the times past. There was a trip to Kew Gardens and two coaches were needed. The annual show profit for the year was noted at £5 19 4d.

1951

In 1951 the membership of the monthly meetings of the VPA improved, there were 38 present in January, 20 present for 'Spraying Pests' and 48 were present at the talk on local birds, the last subject obviously proving very popular, as it has done in recent years. The show unfortunately had rain for the first time, but to everyone's delight still made a proft of £9 16 4d

A challenge cup, which was given by Mr Norman and Mrs Edna Bishop, involved nominated competitions between Church End and East End. In 1951 a tug of war - the first of these competitions - was waged between the two sides and East End carried off the cup. What has happened to the old rivalry, and what has happened to the Challenge Cup?!

1952

1952 was a sad year for the country and for Paglesham WI as well. In February, the country mourned the death of King George VI and, in December, Paglesham WI mourned the passing of its president, Mrs Perry, who had presided last at the Garden meeting at South Hall on June the 4th. The WI showed its sorrow by standing in silence at its meeting.

There had been worry at the July WI meeting of proposals to use Potton Island for explosive experimental work, much discussion occurred and protests were made through the appropriate channels to the Ministry of Agriculture, after a resolution was passed denouncing the proposed experiments.

1953

The last night of January 1953 and the first few days of February brought further sorrow to Paglesham and the surrounding area, for they were the nights and days of the flood of 1953. Mr Boardman reported the breaching of the wall at East End at 12.30am and by 1pm others were moving their sheep and cattle to higher ground, for the walls at Church End had also succumbed to the vicious tide. In all, 600 acres were to be under water in the area, including Waterside Lane and the road at Church End. At the bottom of Waterside Lane, where the boat-building sheds of Frank Shuttlewood were flooded, rowing boats were used as a means of transport. However, Paglesham fared well compared to its neighbours, families and friends on Foulness, who spent days of agony and bereavement while waiting for rescue from the sea which had engulfed their island homes. It was 30 hours before the first people were taken off Foulness and Paglesham inhabitants played their brave part in reaching the Island by boat and rescuing women and children. Mr Douglas 'Biff' Rayner received the MBE for his courage during the rescue work, bringing great honour to the area.

The WI meeting in the hall in February recorded the great shock of the flood disaster. However, life continued and it was decided that this year a harvest supper would be held in the Mission Room and guests would be invited.

The WI harvest supper is still a delight at Paglesham and until the last few years, the WI members totally catered for the whole evening, each being allocated food to bring. The room is cleaned and flowers installed and on Friday afternoon the tables are laid with white linen and then the

Harvesting at Church End - early 1950s

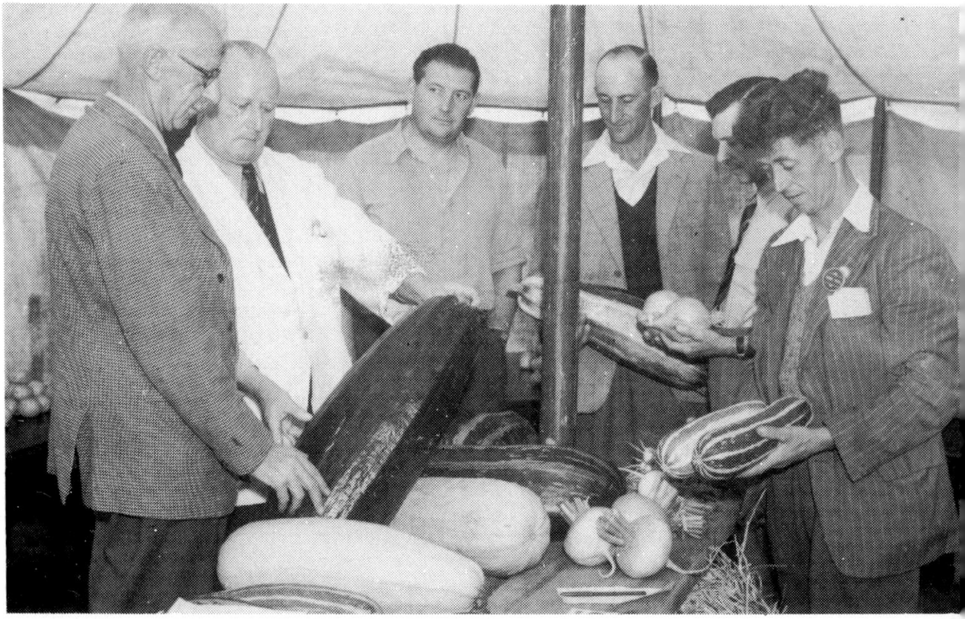

Early VPA Show - c1950

fun begins. Ham, beef, lettuce tomato cucumber, butter in little dishes, big bowls of potato salad, coleslaw, pickle, mustard, salt and pepper all appear. Cider, beer and wine to accompany the meal await the evening, when other members will bring cheese, the Paglesham trifle and, in the past, their own cutlery. When everyone is satisfied that all that can be done has been done, the hall is left with a prayer that the mice are away for the day.

At 7pm, the hall is opened and from 7.30 Madam President receives her guests with a glass of dry or sweet sherry and there is much hilarity, with everyone dressed in their best for the occasion. At 8pm, the Master of Ceremonies for the evening calls the guests to order and asks that they will take supper with the Paglesham WI and its President. One gentleman from each table helps the rest to drinks and everyone tucks in. It is noticeable that people drift to the same table each year for comfort and also to make sure that they have a favourite trifle near them. However, by the end of the evening, the men have sampled most of the trifles as they are passed around.

Once everyone has had sufficient, the tables are cleared and the Master of Ceremonies takes over for games of musical chairs, word games, paper games and quizzes. Many entertainers, including two hilarious singers whose memory still brings tears to many an eye, have given their all at these evenings. From time to time, the WI members and friends have performed plays, or sketches, or songs, and given great delight to themselves, and usually to the audience. Now a 40 year old tradition, may the harvest supper long remain as part of Paglesham culture.

The VPA committee during 1953 had allocated £9 12 0d to VPA members at Church End whose allotments had been flooded during the year. The committee increased its female representation to three ladies and the annual subscription was raised from 1s 6d to 2s per household. A licenced bar was proposed for the summer show by Mr Vic Cardy and, of course, the motion was passed.

During June, the village celebrated the coronation of Queen Elizabeth II with a village pageant. The villagers, 72 in all, enacted small scenes depicting life through the ages. Much of the day was spent watching the coronation on a hired television (black and white in those days), in the school. It was a wet day but things brightened with a comic football match, dance and bonfire in the evening. The challenge cup for 1953 was a darts match held at the Mission Room and I am sure there is someone in the village who will remember who won even though it is not recorded.

Pumping away flood water, Vic Cardy and son - 1953

VPA Prizewinners, 1957

1954

In 1954, the WI formed a drama group which met in the Mission Room regularly. Whist drives were also held by the VPA, bringing in a handsome annual profit of £14. Monthly meetings of the VPA included film shows, talks on 'Travel abroad' and 'Flowers in season'.

The VPA elected its first president that year, in the person of Mr George Perry, of South Hall, and many dignatories of the village have followed in his footsteps. Each president is remembered with affection for the way they stamped their own personality on the revered post. Vice-presidents were also introduced to the VPA and numbered eight in that first year. Mr Derrick Wood became the chairman and would remain so for the next 14 years, a record which surely will remain unbeaten.

The Annual show made a profit of 1d, but the Association had increased its funds in hand to £70 8 7d. Mrs Killick produced a set of new curtains for the hall and the WI at its meetings expressed much worry about the Government proposals of putting a new atomic power station on an Essex river. It was known that Paglesham had been surveyed as a possible site. However, fortunately, because of the small amount of water in the river Roach, the plan was rejected and in 1956, Paglesham heaved a sigh of relief as Bradwell became the target.

1955

In 1955, First Aid lectures were held in the hall weekly from October to November, 7 - 8 people being present each time. It was noted that 7 entered for the examination in November, however, there is no record of how many passed!

1956

By 1956 the VPA committee had developed and now contained half men and half women. A dahlia and chrysanthemum show was held at the hall in September. At the AGM in October, Mrs Ducker was congratulated for her success at the summer show and by setting such high standards for she had won the championship cup three years in a row. She was said to be encouraging keen competition and by 1958 the VPA had made her the first lady VPA secretary.

1957

The ladies of the WI embroidered the green WI tablecloth in 1957, which is still in use today. Miss Harris retired from the committee, and a WI-run whist drive was held in aid of Hungarian Relief.

Mrs Griew was elected to the 'Sanitation sub-committee' of the Mission Room, but it was thirty years before the hall had its own washing-up facilities or a loo.

Prize-giving for the VPA was held separately from the AGM, at an open evening with Mr and Mrs Colebrook at Buckland House. At the AGM, there was lengthy discussion on the price of teas at the summer show, which was considered by some to be *"unrealistic"*. It was felt that members were subsidising all the tea drinking of visitors to that event!

1958

The Mission Room received coats of paint inside and out by Chris and George Popplewell in 1958. The WI still continued its monthly meetings and the talks included 'Care of the feet', ' Wine making' and 'Decorating sponges'. A play about Hard-Apple Blyth, the famous Paglesham smuggler, was performed at the Garden meeting, with Mrs Daphne Wood taking the title role.

The VPA hired side-shows for the summer show from the Kursaal and recorded a profit for the event of 6s 0d! The chrysanthemum and dahlia show made £5 5 0d. There were also debates on such controversial subjects as *"The village of Paglesham is lovely, gay and doomed"*, and *"Highly mechanised farming is a disadvantage to the community"*.

The people of Paglesham decided that the Parish Council, which had met in the hall after the war, was not needed and this of course made the newspaper headlines, Paglesham being the only parish without a parish council in the country. Paglesham was news, not for the first time, and not for the last. Pressure was exerted. The 'media', including Fyfe Robertson, arrived and left. But Paglesham stuck by its decision, and the Parish Council was not reformed until 1964, when one of its main achievements was the provision of several street lights.

1958 also saw the end of two out of three of the church bells which were badly cracked. The third one was repaired and is now rung, at times, to call worshippers to church.

1959

In 1959, Mr Derrick Wood, of The Chase, under the auspices of the VPA, organised the first of a number of trips abroad. A party visited the bulb fields in Holland, and flew from Southend Airport. A small early show was also suggested for May, for the spring flowers, and this continues today to everyone's joy. Rosemary Roberts, nee

A snowy scene - the road past the Mission Room - 1958

WI Harvest Supper in the Mission Room - 1959

Boardman, having married and moved away, became the first associate member. During the late 1950s a men's club was formed which met in the hall, where they played billiards and board games. There were again worries regarding the school's closure, but these proved unfounded.

THE SIXTIES

1960

In 1960, it was noted that there were 694 entries in that summer's show which compares with 457 in 1992.

1961

In 1961, the VPA ran whist drives, films shows and a quiz against the WI. The spring show that year had 50 entries and made a loss of £1 5 1d. Geoffrey Bradley asked for talks to be given to the VPA on floral art. As many of us to our joy today know, this request has produced one of our most delightful and talented floral artists and his flowers have since graced many a hearth and wedding and grave side not only in Paglesham but all over Essex, and even as far as Wales!

1962

In 1962 the VPA and WI worked together at a barbecue to raise money for a school swimming pool for the children, which was later built at Doggetts school. The VPA held whist drives and social evenings at the hall, a dance for the young folk and an evening for the old. The floral art talks began and it is certain that Geoffrey was there to the forefront. The spring show had 89 entries, the summer show, 640, and the dahlia and chyrsanthemum show, 139.

1963

1963 brought ice floes again to the Roach, last seen in 1947. Paglesham shivered but survived and the old hall stood up to the cold. Winter lectures by the VPA were discontinued due to the low attendances and so was the spring show. The VPA and WI bought chairs for the room.

1964

In 1964, Biff Rayner was elected president at the VPA AGM held at the hall. Heating was also discussed and Mr Danny Ball, of Winton Haw, recommended calor gas, which he had installed, and which continues in use today. There was a general discussion about the availability of the hall and

VPA Supper at the Plough and Sail - 1960

Regulars in the Plough & Sail - late 1960s
Vic Cardy, Walter Wood, Bill Robinson, Wopper Staines

many felt that perhaps a new hall ought to be considered. From then to 1976, no meetings of the VPA were held at the hall. The VPA flourished at various venues and it was noted in 1964 that Mark and Rosemary Roberts gave their first historical talk to the VPA AGM, entitled 'Old Paglesham'.

1965

In 1965 Mr Danny Ball, of Winton Haw, Church End, decided to provide some entertainment for the boys and girls of the village and the hall became the home for a group of boys and girls building canoes, playing darts, skittles and shove-ha'penny and listening to pop music.

1966

England won the World Cup in 1966, and the drop in the entries to the summer show, to 270, was blamed on the distraction of the preliminary matches and the cup final

A piano was hired from Gilberts of Southend on the occasion of an old peoples' party at Church Hall Farm. A barn dance also held there caused controversy over the price of hot dogs! The charge of one shilling was considered by some to be far too dear.

1967/8

In 1967 the WI bought new tablecloths for the hall, but the next year, when a president and secretary could not be found, the WI nearly folded. However, Mrs Griew and Mrs Ducker were persuaded to take the posts, and the WI survived.

1969

1969 brought a new worry. Forces gathered, under the leadership of Mr Derrick Wood, to fight the Government's proposal of an airport at Foulness. That would have meant great changes to Paglesham. A long hard case was fought with much evidence being collected and given to the Roskill Commission. Contrary to the findings of Roskill, the Government still decided on Foulness as the proposed site. Parish Councils and others fought on as 'The Defenders of Essex', under the chairmanship of Derrick Wood, and eventually won the day; Paglesham lived on as the village it is today.

Mrs Anfilogoff, founder member and first president of the Paglesham WI, died in 1969, and her death was announced at the monthly meeting. There was still worry of the school closing down, as it now had only 38 pupils.

THE SEVENTIES

1970

Dutch Elm disease, a fungus carried by a beetle, struck many of the elm trees which were part of the character of the area. By 1970 many of the trees were dead and had to be felled. As a consequence the village lost many of its old landmarks. Again Paglesham became world-wide news as residents, old and young, climbed trees to protest against the wholesale cutting down of all elms. Eventually the disease spread, and although elm hedges remain in a few places, the leafy character of our lanes has disappeared.

By now, the mechanisation of farming was universal. The increasing size of combines and other equipment meant that it was more economical for farmers to have larger fields. The scenary also changed with the introduction of new crops, and the open views were splashed with yellow in early summer as oilseed rape became common. More recently, at the end of the 1980s, the shimmering blue of linseed, also grown for its oil, has tinted a number of fields. In 1993, farmers had to 'set aside' a sixth of their acreage, so that some fields were left uncultivated, a sad sight.

Mechanisation also needed fewer farm workers, and many men had to find other work in Rochford, or at Baltic Wharf on Wallasea, or indeed further afield. This was a problem on a national scale, with villagers moving out to find jobs. In 1993, we have only three farmers and three farm workers living and working in the village. But we are very fortunate in the number of long established families still here.

The WI tea in March of 1971 had to be made on the old oilstove as there was a power cut, but only 12 members were present and it is hoped that it did not prove too difficult.

1972

1972 brought the centenary of the school and great celebrations were planned by the teachers and adults alike. A pageant was held at Church Hall barn, with dances and sketches by the children and adults. 600 were in the audience on the day of July 15th and every mother and father was very proud of their offspring. Mr Dye organised the adults, while Mrs Sime, headteacher, with the help of Mrs Rosemary Amis (assistant teacher) and Mrs Daphne Wood (an erstwhile actress and a great supporter of village thespian talent), produced a wonderful performance from her

pupils. A successful dance was held in the evening. Mrs Sime sadly retired a week later.
It was this year also that Rosemary Roberts wrote her first book, 'Paglesham', to much acclaim, and Geoffrey Bradley gave his first recorded floral demonstration to the WI - the first of many that he would bring to the Mission Room.

1974

In 1974 the room was decorated, once more for Christmas and for the WI meeting. A Christmas tree again graced the hall and each member received a small gift from the tree, a custom revived from the past. As always the meeting finished with a carol.

1975

Excitement was generated in Paglesham in the year of 1975 with the WI deciding to enter the Essex Show co-operative class. For this year and the next three years Miss Valerie Thompson and Mrs Thompson made and decorated the WI birthday cake.

The first mention is made of the 'Paglebridge Singers' in 1975. This was a group of women from Paglesham and Stambridge started by Mrs Betty Davies, who also composed the clever and humourous ditties which they sang. The Group especially remembers 1977 when the Paglebridge singers performed at Chelmsford Cathedral, and also the occasion in London in aid of the Society for the Protection of Ancient Buildings, where they went by invitation of the Duke of Grafton. These songs and their words are still appropriate today, judging by the welcome given to them in 1993 at the Diamond Jubilee of Paglesham WI held at Lambourne Hall, Canewdon, the home of Mr and Mrs Roy Cottis. Mrs Davies has retired and the Group has disbanded, but the memories and songs live on.

Miss Winnie Keeble, a member of the WI for many years, celebrated her 80th birthday at the hall with more than 30 members of her family. Some still live in Paglesham, as the Keeble family has since the 1860s.

1976

By 1976 the VPA had rejoined the WI in using the Mission Room for its meetings. Thoughts were put forward to the Church for redecoration but funds were short. Two whist drives, two bingo evenings and children's parties were organised there by the VPA. The reinstated spring show was also held in the hall.

A new Youth Club was formed by Zoe Massey, at which adults,

in the guise of Joan Johnson and Maureen Warren, assisted. The children, as in previous years, played table tennis and board games and had barbecues on the sea wall. In later years, Rex Berrecloth, Jim Rand, Chris Jones and Dave Hatton supervised snooker and card games for some time.

Paglesham held its own street market in 1976 in the Chaseway. Its aim was to raise money for conversion of the school house into a craft room for the school children. At the market there were crafts, antiques, book stalls and homemade cakes and despite it being the beginning of December, the weather was good and many picked up bargains.

1977

The Queen's Silver Jubilee year of 1977 was celebrated with great love and affection country wide. Paglesham did her Majesty proud, crowning the village with bunting from East End, to Jubilee Cottages, to Church End. There was a fancy dress tea at the school, a sports day at Finches and Maules and a sponsored walk organised by the youth club. A barn dance at the Plough and Sail was also held. In their own inimitable way, Ken and Hazel Oliver invited the children for a party in the car park the following Sunday and the excited faces of the children will long remain in the hearts of many of us.

It was also in this year that Mrs Griew wrote to the Ministry of Agriculture with reference to a piece of land that they were selling as part of the National Vegetable Research Station. After much toil by her, the village bought the piece of land opposite East Hall Cottages for a play ground for the children and venue for the village.

Thoughts of a new hall recurred but the cost was too high, and the old Mission Room breathed again. It still greeted the WI and the VPA at their meetings including the spring show and the AGMs. The VPA summer show moved round the village, sometimes East End and sometimes Church End. During the late 70's and 80's Mr Rayner generously made his barns available for the show and the following dance, which was a major fund-raiser. Marquees had become too expensive at £1000 to hire, but the show went from strength to strength and sometimes was large with many craft stalls and sometimes a small village show with a few stalls and games.

In recent years, a marquee has been kindly provided free by Mr Graham and Mrs Rosemary Lintott, previously of Winton Haw, and the summer shows have been held in the Garden Field opposite the Plough, by kind permission of Mrs Phyllis Boardman. This has given a traditional feel to the village's main event of the year, which is much appreciated by the large numbers who attend from far and wide.

The quality of entries in the show has improved so much and great praise has been heaped on the entrants by the judges. Still the pride and joy is shown in the faces of all the winners. Many have been participating and working to make the VPA what it is, from its conception to now. The minutes of the meetings from the first, mention the names of Lol Bradley, Vin Wood, and Dick Thorogood, who have organised shows through the years and continue today with advice, enthusiasm and stewardship.

1978

In the late 1970s, the Church tower caused concern as pieces of stone were falling on the roof of the nave. Fund-raising, that perennial village activity, commenced. A 'Country Day', with sheep shearing, horseshoeing, and many other crafts, was held at Redcroft in June. This was the fore-runner of many events over the next years, including three large craft fairs in East Hall barns, which were organised by Rosemary Roberts in 1981-83. The money raised and anticipated, together with grants and loans, were sufficient to get work under way in 1980.

1979

In 1979 the WI splashed out and bought new cups and saucers and plates for their monthly meetings. Since that time,

Miss Winnie Keeble's 80th Birthday, Mission Room - 1975

the delicate white china with gold WI inscription has become the pride of the ladies, for they all agree that *"there is nothing like a cup of tea from a china cup"*.

Each WI meeting, in fact, is such a joy to behold for the hall is cleaned a day or two before and each of the tables is laid with a starched white cloth, a jar of flowers, napkins and plates. Three different ladies carry out the cleaning, provide sandwiches and cakes for each meeting and take care of the other members. The ladies do this in rotation so each gets a chance to be cossetted. To see the delicate sandwiches and selection of pastries is a matter of pride for everyone who has been a member of the Paglesham WI and long may it continue.

Each meeting has a speaker or film and competition including a best flower. This is followed by the inevitable Paglesham raffle. The meetings are our salute to past values and it is wonderful to snatch just a few hours a month to sit and enjoy and forget the hurly burly of the outside world and slip into shades of the past.

THE EIGHTIES

1980 - 1984

The 1980's arrived in Paglesham bringing many events.

The ladies of the village (plus both authors' husbands) embroidered kneelers which Rev Norman Kelly, the Rector since 1957, blessed at a special service in the church, when the rebuilding of the battlements of the church tower was complete.

Paglesham church, with its tiny congregation, always finds it hard to make ends meet. The money asked for by the diocese has risen from £4 12s 0d in 1946, to £1100 today. The church is one of the few which is always open, and the donations from the many visitors help considerably to its solvency. However, special needs for the fabric require extra efforts.

Apart from the craft fairs mentioned before, a series of nine 'History with Flowers' exhibitions in the church, organised by Rosemary Roberts over the next dozen years, helped repay the debts, and start a fund for the remaining repairs, which were not then so urgent. On these occasions, the church was decked with **flower arrangements**, as well as displays of, for example, a **wartime room**, Victorian costume, always put on by **Mrs Ann Boulter**, and other exhibits of local interest.

The wedding of Prince Charles and Lady Diana Spencer in 1981 was celebrated at East Hall barns with a tea and barn dance.

Paglesham twinned with La Boissière École, a small village south west of Paris near Rambouillet. Exchange trips were organised by Leo and Margie Massey and the first visit of the French to Paglesham is still remembered. In its usual fashion, Paglesham rolled out the red carpet and greeted them with a cold supper and barn dance in East Hall barn on the Saturday night. The mounds of rice salad and the effect of the French wine that our guests brought with them are still remembered. The French adopted Dick Thorogood and his bowler hat as their mascot during these visits and eventually they raffled his bowler hat. On return visits we were treated royally and many a tear was shed at each parting and many a story is told of the villagers' antics under the influence of the vin du pays!

A health survey of the village was held by Dr.Angela Puzey in 1980 as a forerunner of the Government's aim to give everyone regular health checks. People came and enjoyed having themselves weighed, their blood pressure taken, smoking and drinking habits chided and their water tested. The old Mission Room had never seen anything quite like it before!

VPA Childrens party - 1983

VPA 40th Anniversary photo - 1986

WI meeting - 1986

Rochford Day Centre was opened in the 80's and a bus was kindly provided by the Centre to pick up Paglesham pensioners on a Tuesday. It still takes them into Rochford to the Market, and the shops and they have a good lunch at the Day Centre; usually four or five people make the journey. Paglesham, in return, helps to raise money for the centre, holding the occasional coffee morning at the hall and donating money from a whist drive each year, for which the centre is very grateful. The weekly trip to Rochford is some of the villagers' only outing, and is very dear to their hearts.

It was in these days also that Joan Johnson and Angela Puzey approached the vicar about the WI managing the hall, as the hall was making a loss. These two ladies felt that they could bring about improvement and profit. Rev Kelly agreed and the Mission Room has never looked back; cupboards and a new sink were installed by Ian Puzey, Geoff Wooding, Fred Petchey and Chris Jones. Beautiful new whist tables were made by Mick Young and Albert Mountney and these were bought by the VPA. Monthly whist drives were introduced, with Dick Thorogood as master of ceremonies.

With the help of the Parish Council, who were now meeting regularly at the hall, under the umbrella of the Roach Group (Barling, Wakering Foulness and Paglesham) formed in 1973, money was raised for toilets. The work was undertaken by Ted Thorogood and Brian Sharp. The hall had outside lights added and a coat of paint in 1987. Then Ken and Hazel Oliver with their usual kindness donated a carpet taken out of the Plough and Sail which originally came from Tots, a nightclub in Southend. Altogether the hall became a delight to observe - and the new conveniences were a great blessing.

WI meetings continued in their new surroundings and the ladies could now have an extra cup of tea, as toilet facilities were present and they did not have visit a nearby house as they had done in the past.

For the Golden Jubilee of the Paglesham WI in 1983, the hall was twice decorated with daffodils, both at the tea party for the WI which followed lunch at the Plough and Sail, and at the spring show later. Each of the WI Members had a wonderful Golden Jubilee day and the room rang with their laughter and joy, a little of it undoubtedly due to the sherry. The birthday cake was cut by Mrs Ducker, the only founder member present, and the president, Mrs Molly Bell.

Weekly art classes began at this time, and still flourish. Many a Monday night sees the room awash with oils and water colours, attracting students from Canewdon and Hawkwell, as well as Paglesham folk, the ages ranging from 20 to 83 years old. New pupils who have never lifted a paintbrush, at least since youth, blossom over the months under expert tutelage. Coffee is provided and sometimes at a birthday or special occasion we celebrate with wine and delicacies. Geraldine Warren taught the art class for many years, and Rodney Choppin has now taken over this fine work. Both the whist and the art class are a great support to the Mission Room funds from the profits made and fees charged.

The school eventually closed in 1984. Only 14 children remained when the sad tidings were announced. It was inevitable and the battle was finally lost 37 years after the first threats. Its history is told in Rosemary Roberts' second book on the village 'The Children of Paglesham', published in 1990.

1985 -1989

1985 saw the closing of the only remaining shop in Paglesham. For a while the Post Office was run at the Mission Room before going to East Hall cottages with Val McVittie until 1992. Now the nearest one is at Stambridge.

When Joan Johnson moved from the village, Mrs Nan Peel, with great expertise, continued with Angela Puzey to run the Mission Room. The hall was well used and a blessing to the village for without the school, life revolved around the Mission Room, as it really always has over the last hundred years.

The VPA and WI have bought new folding tables and crockery which people borrow for a small fee. Each late March or April, the VPA spring show still graces the hall. It is a shower of gold from the daffodils and everyone delights in the intoxicating perfume of the hyacinths. Each year there is still much discussion on the length of trumpet and petals of the various blooms.

VPA suppers are still held in the Plough and Sail, with Ken and Hazel Oliver and son Mark as our hosts. They cater wonderfully for 60 to 80 people each December, with a starter, cold meats and salad, a choice of sweet, and cheese. Everyone is made so welcome, and the Olivers triumph each year. Throughout the year they give their all for the village with many good deeds, never publicised, to help the smooth-running of village life.

Over the years, the VPA has held numerous events to encourage interest: Carnival parades at the beginning of the summer show, when 'Spanish ladies', 'dragons' and 'nuns in Wellington boots' marched through the village; Boule days at Cupola House, organised by Jeremy and Alison

Zabell; Sailing days, by Gordon Warren; Fun days with swimming, archery, fishing, conversation etc at Winton Haw, by Ken and Pat Gage; Treasure Hunts round the village, by Alan Hoskins and Mark Roberts; and a never-to-be- forgotten music-hall; individual days, and scenes, which we will remember for years to come.

These days elections are another source of money for the Mission Room as the District Council takes over the hall as a Polling Station for the day, bringing its own toilet, until ours was installed. Church End and Jubilee vote at the chapel now that the school has been closed. There are so few people at East End, that tellers must sit most of the day alone, waiting for the odd person to stroll in; however, we try to make it as interesting as possible for them by spreading ourselves out throughout the day!

The hurricane in 1987 brought great damage to the village. A night of fear and destruction saw trees falling all around us. Slates came off roofs, chimneys came down, walls collapsed and the roof of the hall was displaced. To see the cherished hall with its roof twisted, windows smashed and dirt abounding, seemed like adding disaster to disaster.

With usual aplomb the people of Paglesham responded, the room was cleared, the Insurance contacted and all was put to rights by the village builders, Ted Thorogood and Brian Sharp. Inside and out looked as good as new within a few weeks, with sparkling new paint and only a couple of meetings had to be cancelled.

It had taken five days to restore telephone and electricity to Paglesham but a lot longer to mend broken roofs and cut up the fallen trees, as in many other parts in South East England, after that nightmare weekend.

A small fire in East End Paglesham interrupted a WI meeting in the hall in 1988 as Mrs Alex Donald, an old inhabitant of Paglesham and widow of Professor Ian Donald, the pioneer of ultra sound for pregnant women, tried manfully to give her talk on 'Christmas in Sweden'. Numerous members took to their heels, feeling that they might be needed to help with the fire. However the fire was small, damaging a shed and fence, and the meeting continued, despite all.

In the late 80's and early 90's the hall prospered and a new car park was constructed to allow for parking off the road. Parking was becoming quite a serious problem for older members of the WI who came from a distance by car, and also for the night visitors to the hall. An exchange

Bazaar in aid of Mission Room Funds - 1990

Art Exhibition, Mission Room - 1992

of land has recently been completed with Biff Rayner, so that there is more space available behind the Mission Room for the future. Evening events now include a cricket supper and a sailing club supper.

Linda Berrecloth formed a mother and toddler group in 1989 and this met at the Mission Room room once a week on a Thursday. At one point there were nine mothers and children, however, as the children have gone to school, the group stopped and there is no longer the joy of seeing the tiny chairs and toys. Maybe in the future we can hope for the toddler group's return.

Children started to have their parties in the hall and some have even held 18th and 21st parties there. Lol and Gwen Bradley, who had their Wedding reception in the hall in 1939, had another reception there for their Golden Wedding in 1989.

RECENT YEARS

The Paglesham Parish Council, under the chairmanship of Mr Ian Puzey since the amicable dissolution of the Roach Group in 1991, meets in the hall every few months, airing its business on street lighting and footpaths to a few loyal villagers , unless of course there is some topic which fires the imagination, when a larger gathering attends.

The VPA has its committee meetings there and in the early 90s organised a Christmas bazaar when all the users of the hall participated to raise funds. Father Christmas in many guises, male and female, attended to listen to requests from the children and caused great merriment.

The art class held its first exhibition in December 1992 and the walls of the hall were hung lovingly with the artists' work of the previous year, with local crafts on sale as well. The food was good, the wine was flowing, the entry was free and the room was full. Many of the artists experienced the pride and joy of admiration of their work, for the first time.

The monthly whist drives are still very popular, at times incorporating eight tables. The one in the week before Christmas attracts even more people, with mince pies and sausage rolls replacing the usual coffee and biscuits, and even bigger prizes abound. It is a joy to see the older inhabitants, who sometimes do not see many people throughout the week, chatting with the young and middle aged folk and participating in their joys and worries.

The WI, the hall's stalwart guests through all its years,

remains loyal with its monthly meetings. Over the last years during the winter months, Sunday church services with Rev Kelly, our Rector since 1957, have been held in the hall, so the Mission Room rings again with the sound of familiar old hymns.

Stone falling from the west window of the church tower, in 1993, revived fund-raising for that uncompleted task. As it was the 110th anniversary of the restoration of the church in 1883, there was a special commemmoration service, with descendants of Zachary Pettitt and the Wiseman family attending. Another historical exhibition was held at the same time. Thanks to Biff Rayner, who regularly cuts the graveyard grass, and to Ken Gage, Geraldine and Barry Champ and others, who strimmed, vacuumed and painted, the church and its surroundings looked exceptionally smart.

Other fund-raising events for the tower this year included two talks with slides, in the Mission Room, about the 1953 floods, given by Mark and Rosemary Roberts, a skiff-launching by Gordon Warren, a breakfast by Alan and Sue Hoskins, a farm walk organised by Brian Fletcher, and a progressive dinner arranged by David and Sue Whittingham. This has been a splendid effort in the true Paglesham tradition of rallying round when help is needed.

In the last few months a new Mission Room committee, led by Angela Puzey and Nan Peel, with representatives from all societies that use the hall, has been established. The hall can now progress from strength to strength and the workload of raising money and responsibility for the room in future years will be shared.

This year of 1993 sees the centenary of the hall. In time for the celebrations, the outside was painted in late July by Brian Sharp and Mick Young, including the galvanised, corrugated steel roof that was renewed last year. Volunteers, under the direction of Ken Gage, John Holliday and Ian Puzey, then set to and attacked the inside and now that, too, is a joy to behold.

On the weekend of the 4th/5th September, the village will remember its past with a Victorian weekend. As in the last three years, the 'Summer Show and Fete' will be held in a marquee in the 'Garden Field' on the Saturday, while a Craft Fair will be held there on the Sunday. Afterwards, the village will gather for a special Paglesham tea, recalling the one held 100 years ago, when our benefactor, Zachary Pettitt, presented the Mission Room to the village. The Mission Room itself will have a small service of thanksgiving, and house, appropriately, an exhibition of 'A Century of Paglesham Life'.

WI 60th Celebration - 1993

*Mr Ian Puzey, Proof Reader and Mr Mark Roberts, Editor
at a Music Hall Evening - 1990*

POSTSCRIPT

We are often asked how Paglesham has changed. The buildings have altered less than in many other places, although several houses have been demolished, some not replaced. However, there were more 'new' houses in 1893 than there are now, but today, most of the cottages and large houses have been modernised, with the services that urban dwellers expect, and many houses have been extended to provide the space demanded for today's lifestyle.

The people have changed, too, few working in the village now that the oyster trade has gone and farming is mechanised. Families are considerably smaller, and this is reflected in the halving of our population. There are more retired people in the village. Mobility is greater for almost all - while London was accessible to the Wisemans, many can now travel the world. Our children have ambitions and achievements inconceivable to the Victorians. Despite these differences, one constant is the sense of community.

The glimpses of life in Paglesham over a hundred years, the attitudes of the nineteenth century changing with the decades, have hopefully put the hectic urban-oriented lifestyle of today into some perspective.

Life in a village is always changing, and we tend to fear that the end of Paglesham as we know it is at hand. However, looking back over a century shows that while eras come and go, and families change, new people arrive to take up the challenge of adapting to the present day.

Our village hall has seen many changes over the years, but its use remains a great joy to the people of Paglesham. It is still, after a century, an essential part of village life and we give many thanks to Mr Zachary Pettitt.

SOURCES

History of the Rochford Hundred, Paglesham, by Philip
    Benton (1883)
Diaries of Frederick and Rosalind Wiseman (1887-1897)
Kelly's Directories (1890-1912)
Census data (1891-1931)
Victoria County History, Essex Vol 2 (1907)
Paglesham Primary School Log Books (1910-1968) ERO E/ML96
Diaries of Miss Zillah Harris (1915-1960)
Paglesham Women's Institute Minute Books (1933-1993)
Paglesham Village Produce Association Minute Books
    (1946-1993)
Paglesham, by Rosemary Roberts (1972)
The Children of Paglesham, by Rosemary Roberts (1990)

INDEX OF NAMES

Allen 43
Amis 67
Anfilogoff 39,44,66
Atkinson 33,34
Baldwin 3,44,45
Ball 64,66
Bannister 28
Barnes 35
Beckwith 3
Bell 74
Benton 81
Berrecloth 69,78
Bishop 56
Blyth 33,62
Boardman 42,45,46,49
  50-3,57,63,64,69
Bond Cover,14,30,38
Boulter 71
Bowen 43,52
Bradley 47,52,64,68
  70,78
Bright 51
Brown 24,35,36,48
Browning 3,15,24
Cardy 47,48,59
Chamberlain 45,46
Champ 79
Charles, Prince 72
Choppin 17,24,75
Clark 6
Coe 3
Colebrook 62
Cottis 68
Cousins 33
Dannatt 25
Davies 68
Dixon .44
D'Oisy, Marquis 46
Donald 76
Ducker 40,54,56,61
  66,74
Dye 67
Ellis 40,54
Edward VII King 30
Edward VIII King 44
Elizabeth 2 Qn.53,59
Fance 47
Farthing 35
Fletcher 44,47,52,79
Fraser 31,35,38
Fuller 13
Gage 76,79
Galpin 39
Garon 47
George V King 14,30
  43,44

George VI King 57
Grafton, Duke of 68
Gilbert 66
Griew 62,66,69
Groves 37
Hall 15,19
Hargreaves 13
Harris 9,10,29,36,37
  39,41,43,46,48
  49,51,52,61,81
Hatton 69
Hill 3
Himler 50
Hines 47
Hitler 45,46,49
Hobby 5
Holliday 79
Hoskins 76,79
Hutley 5,23,45
James 3
Jennings 38,43-45
  48,49
Johnson 69,74,75
Jones 69,74
Keeble 22,38,47,50
  52,68,70
Kemp 2,3,22,27,41-43
  47,52
Kelly 71,74,79,81
Kersteman 4
Killick 47,54,61
King 29
Kitchener 36
Lapwood 51
Lea 2,3,5,6,12,31
Leach 9
Leavett 9
Lintott 69
Loader 49,55
Lucking 54,56
Luker 20
Martin 43,45,49
Massey 68,72
May 42
McBriar 53
McVittie 75
Meeson 29,35,43
Miller 19
Mortier 1
Mountney 74
Mussolini 50
Nicholls 6,36,37,43
Noble 25
Norris 44
Olley 19,25
Oliver 69,74,75

Payne 10
Peacock 38
Peel 75,79
Perry 46,57,61
Petchey 74
Pettitt i,1-6,12,13
  15,17,20,22,24,27
  28,29,36,37,45,79
  81
Pizzey 9
Popplewell 15,19,31
  62
Potton 19,37
Powell 35
Puzey 72,74,75,78,79
  80
Quy 2,3,9,10
Rampling 53,54
Rand 69
Rayner 57,64,69,78
  79
Reay 3
Rice 19,34
Roberts 62,66,68,70
  71,75,76,79-81
Roosevelt 46,50
Robertson 62
Sharp 47,74,76,79
Shuttlewood 15,19,24
  37,44,57
Sime 67
Simpson 44
Smeaton 37
Smith 43
Sparrow 13,24
Spencer, Lady D 72
Staines 19
Tawke 40
Thompson 56,68
Thorogood 47,51,52
  55,70,72,74,76
Victoria Queen 5,26
Warren 69,75,76,79
Watkins 53
Whittingham 79
Willans 37
Winterbon 2
Wiseman 1-3,6-9,12
  17,19,20,22,24-28
  31,37,55,79,81,84
Wood 42,46,47,52,61
  62,66,67,70
Wooding 74
Woolf 3,13,29,32
Young 79
Zabell 45,76

82

GENERAL INDEX

Ashingdon 26
Australia 37
Baltic Wharf 67
Barling 74
Barn Row 19
Bedford Row 10
Berlin 51
Blackwall 40
Blue House 10
Boarded Row 19
Boatbuilding 15-17
  19,44,57
Boer War 30
Boissiere Ecole 72
Bowl field 10,44
Brake, see Bus
Bradwell 61
Brick Row 19
Brightlingsea 27
Brighton 40,41
Buckland Cot. 22
Buckland House 8,9
  22,29,37,43,44,46
Bus 27-29,32,33,35
  37-39,55,74
Canada 27
Canewdon 14,38,68,74
Chalkwell 49
Chapel 13,48,76
Charabanc, see Bus
Chase, The 6,21,22
  36,41,44,54
Chaseway Cot. 22,29
Chelmsford 6,68
Chingford 46
Church, The 1,2,4-7
  10-12,29-31,33,35
  37,38,43,44,50,68
  70,71,74,79
Church Hall 5,6,10
  28,290,49,60,67
Clothing 25,26,50,70
Clubs 1,4,41,64,66
  68,74,78
Claverham Cot. 13
Clements 15,28,44
Cobblers Row 19
Colchester 27
Council houses 14
Coursing 29
Creeksea 15,27
Cricket 7,10,29,78
Crouch, River 27
Cupola House 3,5,22
  23,27,45,49,52,54
Cycling 23,31,32,35
Def'ders of Essex 66
Dinners, see Meals
District C'cil 38,76
Droitwich 43
Dutch Elm Disease 66
East Hall 15,24,25
  48,49,69,70,72,75
Endway 19
Entertainments 1,3,13
  14,17,27-29,37,43,45

59,63,66-69,63,66-69
·72,75-77,79,80
Farming 4,5,9,12,13,27
  28,37,42,48,49,51,53
  54,58,67,69,79
Finches (and Maules) 9
  10,12,69
Floods 38,57,60
Foulness 54,57,66,74
France 4
Germany 46
Glenthorpe 24
Grape Vine Cot. 15
Grapnells 5
Great War 31,34-37
Great Tey 3
Hadleigh 7
Haltern 38
Hawkwell 74
Hockley 26
Holland 7,62
Hove To 22
Hullbridge 27
Illust. London News 15
Ingulfs 5,10,13
Italy 46,51
Jubilee Cot 14,69,76
Jubilees 5,6,13,14,43
  69,74
Jutland 36
Kew 56
Kursaal 40,62
Lambourne Hall 68
Leigh 13
Library 37
Loftmans 3-5,13,37,28
London 9,27,28,31,33,68
Lunches, see Meals
Lunts 22,45
Manchester 25
Marine Cot. 6,
Marsh House 19
Mayflower Group 39
Meals 1,2,5,6,8,13,17
  20,22,30,31,40,45,50
  55-57,65,69,71,72,74
  75,78,79
Mersea 9,27
Milton Vil. 19,29,36
Mourning 26,57
New Cot. 42
Newlands 22
New Row 19
New Zealand 49
Nottingham 6
OBS Cot. 24
Ostend 27
Oxford 51
Oysters 3,5-9,15,18,20
  22,27,37,38,43,55
Paris 72
Parish Council 6,45,62
  74,78
Plough and Sail 7,17,19
  20-22,33,39,44,55
  65,69,73,74,75

Plumtree 6
Poland 46
Post (Office) 19,33,75
Potton Island 57
Pound House 24
Pound Pond 7
Punch Bowl 10-13,29,35
  38,58
Rambouillet 72
Rayleigh 9,25
Rector 3,30,31,35,38,49
  71,75
Rectory 5,10,13,29,31,38
Redcroft 9,22,31,37,39
  40,43,70
Rices Row 19
Roach, River 16,61
Roach Group 74,78
Rochford 2,4,5,17,22,27
  29,33,37,38,41,44,48
  49,67,74
Rose Cot. 22,23
Roskill Comm. 66
Scandal Row 19
School 5,13,14,31,37
  38,43,48,53,59,69
  75,76,78
Scotland 19
Shops 5,19,27,33,34,75
Shop Row 19,36
Shore Ends 19
Smugglers Elms 7
Southend 4,20,25-28,36
  47,62,66,74
South Hall 24,25,57
Southminster 27
Stambridge 7,28,32,68,75
Stannetts 3,24,29,50
Suppers, see Meals
Sutton 13
Swatchways 19
Sweden 76
Sweetlips 10
Suffolk 3
Tailors Row 19
Teas, see Meals
Thundersley 39
Tobruk 51
USA 56
Vine Cot. 15
Violin 33
Wakering 74
Wallasea 5,67
Water Rat Hall 19
Waterside Lane 18,41,57
Well House 3,15,19
Westcliff 35,39
West Hall 4,10
Winton Haw 12,64,69,76
Woolfs Cot. 13,32,33
Workhouse 15
Worlds End Cot. 10
World War 1,
  see Great War
World War 2 2,14,24,41
  44,46-51

83

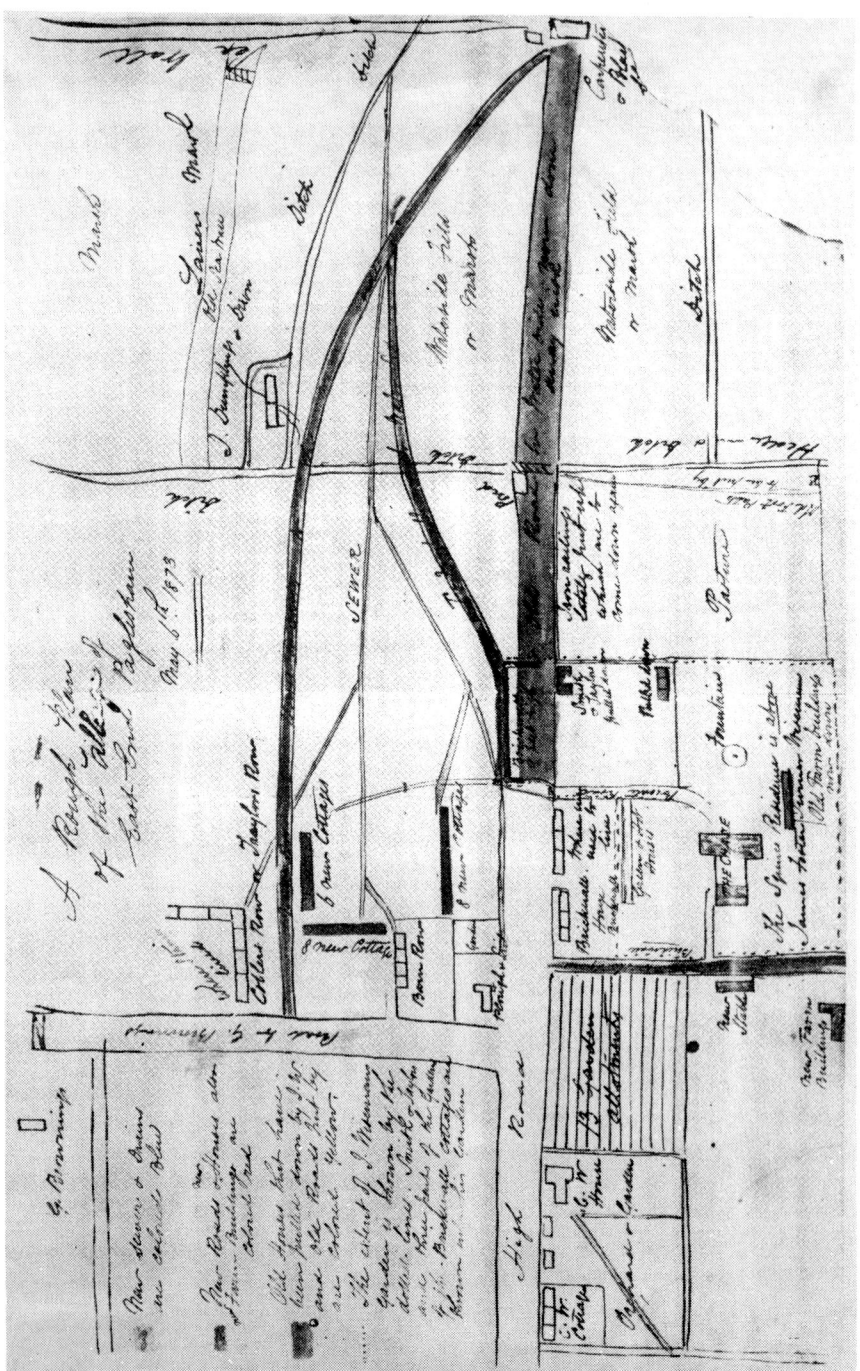

Map by J F T Wiseman, showing changes at East End – 1873